Eighteenth-Century Women Poets

SUNY Series in
Feminist Criticism and Theory

Michelle A. Massé, Editor

Eighteenth-Century Women Poets

Nation, Class, and Gender

Moira Ferguson

STATE UNIVERSITY OF NEW YORK PRESS

Cover illustration courtesy of The Metropolitan Museum of Art, Bequest of Isaac D. Fletcher, 1917. Mr. and Mrs. Isaac D. Fletcher Collection. [17.120.204]

Production by Ruth Fisher
Marketing by Dana E. Yanulavich

Published by
State University of New York Press, Albany

For information, address State University of New York Press, State University Plaza, Albany, NY 12246

Library of Congress Cataloging-in-Publication Data

Ferguson, Moira.
    Eighteenth-century women poets : nation, class, and gender / Moira Ferguson.
        p.   cm. — (SUNY series in feminist criticism and theory)
    Includes bibliographical references (p.).
    ISBN 0–7914–2511–8 (acid-free paper). — ISBN 0–7914–2512–6 (pbk. : acid-free paper)
    1. English poetry—Women authors—History and criticism. 2. Women and literature—Great Britain—History—18th century. 3. Working class writings, English—History and criticism. 4. English poetry—18th century—History and criticism. 5. National characteristics, English, in literature. 6. National characteristics, Scottish, in literature. 7. Collier, Mary—Criticism and interpretation. 8. Scott, Mary, poet—Criticism and interpretation. 9. Yearsley, Ann, 1756–1806—Criticism and interpretation. 10 Little, Janet, 1759–1813—Criticism and interpretation.   I. Title.   II. Series.
    PR555.W6F47   1995
    821'.5099287—dc20   94-47993
                                                                            CIP

10 9 8 7 6 5 4 3 2 1

For
Garnet Larson

CONTENTS

CHAPTER ONE

Introduction

Several laboring-class women sounded themselves into the void in the course of the eighteenth century. This study charts some intersections of gender, class, and national identity in their writings. It questions how national identity might have influenced class and gender affiliations and, reciprocally, how gender determines the nature of nationalism, particularly its redeployment during the revolutionary period (1770–1800) in which most of these texts were written.

The first poet in this lineage, washerwoman Mary Collier, affirms the importance of laboring women and their work in *The Woman's Labour* (1739) while underwriting the growing prominence of English nationalism. In *The Poems of Mary Collier . . . A New Edition*, Collier further introduces a range of political poems that distinguish a gendered class identity for women like herself from that of male laborers. Her varying vantage points partly stem from changes in labor practices. The enclosure of cultivable and common land had severely affected working women like Mary Collier, although the long-term consequences of enclosure evolved gradually. In general, women's traditional functions in the workplace were eroding although women still worked alongside men in the fields;[1] the lives of laboring women remained focused on survival. Collier's experiences as a washerwoman and her description of female field workers were probably accurate for England in the late 1730s.

In terms of her attitude toward the nation, unmarried Collier's praise of the royal family as the quintessential domestic model for Britons locates her in the complex role of a loyal subject who expects women workers to be treated on a par with men. Initially she is responding to laboring poet Stephen Duck's attack in *The Thresher's Labour* on female fecklessness during harvest time. This emergence of forceful poetry by mostly working-class women from the late

1

EIGHTEENTH-CENTURY WOMEN POETS

1730s to the 1790s is part of what Gerald Newman calls "the crucial years in the launching of English [and Scottish] nationalism."[2] In the decades preceding midcentury, when conventional assumptions about church and sovereign rights were dissolving, British people had begun to think about themselves and other nations and communities in new ways.[3] The papacy and allied forms of absolutism, especially royal and aristocratic, were denounced as unacceptable institutions and practices. A Protestantism linked to military patriotism had become a desirable coupling earlier in the century at the accession of George I in 1714, which secured the Hanoverian succession.[4] In John Brewer's words, Protestantism consolidated the nation's preferred self-image as "unified, morally regenerating of ancient Saxon decencies, and forward-looking."[5]

In 1774, Mary Scott's commendatory poem to women, *The Female Advocate*, culturally enhanced this Protestant worldview and national self-perception. A dissenter from Somerset, Scott creatively constructed an intellectual Protestant continuum of female writers. She traces the historical origins of female poets, prose writers, and polemicists, paying tribute to contemporary writers and to neglected as well as eminent predecessors. Scott also reaccentuates the significance of female coteries and scholarship within this recast lineage. Her virtual exclusion of Roman Catholics underscored the prevalent view that the Catholic community consisted of outsiders who created fissures from within.

Scott's concentration on female culture subtly reflects the fact that many middle-class women's lives had assumed a more private and hermetic character. For one thing, eighteenth-century middle-class women who remained single and were not independently wealthy faced a sharply limited choice of occupations. As men worked for the changing economy in an environment separate from their domestic lives, many women turned to marriage as one valuable entrée into adult society, "recommended as an alliance of sense."[6] Mary Scott's reconstruction of a cultural continuum helps to redress the sense of increasing powerlessness generated by the marginalization of bourgeois women in the marketplace.[7] Unlike her feminist predecessor Bathsua Makin, Scott does not simply recite lists of illustrious women whose existence, valor, social class, and intellect could counteract some argument from male authority with one of female authority; rather, she attempts a commendatory and compensatory historical overview. Additionally, the poem remaps the contours of national identity, principally based on the texts of Englishwomen from the middle class and aristocracy. Her inclusion of a slavewoman and a working-class Irishwoman notwithstanding,

Scott negotiates a redefinition of English, middle-class, Protestant culture.

Mary Scott's Protestant vision was shared by a majority of the nation. Such a weltanschauung solidified precarious territorial borders and encouraged Britons to see themselves as a distinct and gifted people who constantly battled for the recovery of lost rights.[8] The growth of industry and commerce enriched this self-image of Britain as an important global force. As if to stress this national claim still further, "Britain" and "Great Britain" had superseded "England" as the names of the nation.[9]

In contrast to a united Protestant nation (that inevitably contained outsiders) was Anglo-French difference. A major commercial and imperial rival for centuries, France had long kindled cross-channel anxieties. France and French people were equated with Roman Catholicism, indolence, fashion, and immorality.[10]

By the 1780s, when the Bristol milkwoman Ann Yearsley's first volume of poems was published, a national culture that manifested some of these assumed characteristics had gradually fashioned itself. Britain was configured as a country that had cherished liberties since Alfred the Great: the people's "free-born" status was unique; the right to self-determination was an English right. A mythology about an ancient democratic social contract had come into being and was playing itself out, although its origins had largely been inherited from the seventeenth century.[11]

Yearsley displays allied concerns about class and gender that echo those of her countrywomen from the provinces, Mary Collier and Mary Scott. Both personal and political considerations explain Yearsley's shift from the more explicitly gynocentric orientation of Collier and Scott. Like Mary Collier, Ann Yearsley was dependent on outside aid for access to publishers. As a case in point, an irreversible dispute with her patron, Hannah More, affected her reputation and, specifically, the publication of her second volume of poems. Yearsley's shadowy presence on the literary scene proved that access to successful publication depended on economics as much as talent—especially for a laboring woman like herself.

Similar factors also clarify Yearsley's francophilic framework in *Earl Goodwin: A Play*, staged at the outbreak of the French Revolution. But by 1793, the milkwoman-poet had introduced gallophobic concerns that stemmed from her son's—as well as England's—military involvement in the revolutionary war. Just as Catholics disrupted the nation from within, so the French disrupted externally. Particularly during this military epoch, Englishness was encoded as the antithesis of Roman Catholicism, foreign aggression, and absolutism. Britons comprised a tough nation—they thought—that exercised sovereign power but within prescribed limits.[12] "Cultural [self-] realization was well under way."[13] The imperial conquest of others and French rivalry generated a relatively fluid national identity.

Ann Yearsley's recently discovered poems in the Bristol Public Library further complicate her radical politics. They highlight her sympathy for Thomas Chatterton's suicide, her desire for domestic order and global harmony. Most of all, they suggest how deeply discomfited she felt about her public representation and confirm that her commitment to patriotism was equivocal at best.

Concurrently with Yearsley, Janet Little uses her volume of poems, published in 1792, to protect a precarious social status and an oppositional nationalist position as a Scottish dairywoman-poet. In a class identification with Mary Collier and Ann Yearsley, Little applauds the talents of her celebrated compatriot, ploughman-poet Robert Burns, just as Mary Collier extols thresher-poet Stephen Duck. Resembling Collier's attitude toward Duck, Little's political as well as personal sentiments toward Burns also destabilize her text. Wary about attacking Scotland's new standard-bearer, she sides with Burns against the ruling elite but censures his free relations with women. The trio of Collier, Yearsley, and Little exemplifies positive laboring-class values and a sense of cultural autonomy.

Yet inevitably, Little's discourse about national identity constitutes itself slightly differently. As a Scottish poet and dairywoman, Little composes an arresting volume of poems that doubles as a gendered, anticolonial testimonial while it subtly disdains class superiors. Her poems, moreover, substantially interact with Robert Burns's life and text. Where Collier, Yearsley, and Scott uphold English liberty as a paramount tenet, Janet Little applauds Scotland and its defiant warriors.

By pondering why the English literati envy Burns, she indirectly challenges a recently constructed English nationalist formulation, avowedly cherished by England's prominent writers. That is to say, she highlights the separation of English and Scottish culture, insisting that Englishness and Scottishness are contested and competing terrains. She thwarts a collective though unconscious English presentation of British culture as homogeneous. Scottish culture, she suggests, requires a distinctly marked definition.

Simultaneously, she quietly demurs at Burns's treatment of women, her sensitivity to gender a notable feature of many poems. Occupying a recognizably Scottish patriotic position, she straddles two discrete and critical antagonisms—Britain versus the world and

England versus Scotland. She speaks from plural vantage points that frequently conflict and overlap.

In that sense, Janet Little is a split subject; she signs an angry working-class woman and, just as importantly, a prideful Scotswoman. Introducing new tropes and figures of alterity that challenge received tenets, she renders a muted belligerent intervention in the national politic while maintaining allegiance to class and gender. Janet Little undermines a subtle praxis of cultural domination, upholding the rights of marginalized communities.

Put another way, despite class and gender alliances, Little plays out a fraught colonial relationship with the trio of English poets, Mary Collier, Mary Scott, and Ann Yearsley. Mapping new contours, she represents and introduces discontinuity, obliquely canceling a popular unitary discourse about Britishness.

Oppositional readings of this quartet of poets, then, sharpens the construction of comparative ethnic identities and the political intricacy of the class and gender axis. Collier, Yearsley, and Little constitute an emerging gendered tradition of working-class poets committed to new formulations of patriotism and national identity, raising significant issues of class and gender as part of that identity. Mary Scott complements and consolidates the trio's innovative discourse by eulogizing middle-class Englishwomen and thereby broadening cultural boundaries. Poetry may be the preferred genre of these poets, but in varied ways they circulate new cultural narratives and their diverse capacities challenge and even block out other, more received chronicles. Eighteenth-century women's poetry, I submit, redefined nation and culture in class and gendered terms.

I have incurred a large number of debts in the course of writing this book. For the chapter on Mary Collier, I thank David Stuart Rodes for helpful comments on an early draft, Patricia Gill, county archivist of the Archive Repository of the West Sussex County Council and of the Diocese of Chichester, for information generously extended, and Sir Alan Lubbock for useful information. An early section of this chapter appeared as the introduction to *The Thresher's Labour, Stephen Duck (1736) and The Woman's Labour, Mary Collier (1739)*, William Andrews Clark Memorial Library, University of California, Los Angeles, 1985.

For kind assistance in tracing Mary Scott, I thank David Bromwich, librarian, Somerset County Library, Local History Library, The Castle, Taunton, Somerset; Hilda M. Massey, Frome, Somerset; Michael McGarvie, also of Somerset; S. G. McKay, social historian of Milborne Port; Margaret De Molte, sub-librarian, Local History

Library, Central Library, Manchester; Derek M. M. Shorrocks, Somerset County Archivist; Dr. Marjorie Reeves of Oxford; Hugh F. Steele-Smith, Ilkley, West Yorkshire; and the Library of the Society of Friends, Friends House, Euston Road, London, especially archivist Malcolm Thomas. Chapter 3 appeared in a different formulation as "'The Cause of My Sex': Mary Scott and the Female Literary Tradition" in *The Huntington Library Quarterly* (Autumn, 1987).

For the chapters on Ann Yearsley, I am indebted to the Bristol Reference Library for permission to quote from Ann Yearsley's unpublished poems and to Dawn Dyer, assistant librarian, who opened up the collection and generously assisted me in tracking down persons and ambiguities in the unpublished poems. I thank Linda Frazier, managing editor of *Tulsa Studies in English Literature*, for invaluable comments.

Part of chapter 4 appeared as "Resistance and Power in the Life and Writings of Ann Yearsley" in *The Eighteenth Century: Theory and Interpretation* (Fall, 1986). A version of the essay on Ann Yearsley's unpublished poems appeared as the introduction to a facsimile edition of these poems in *Tulsa Studies in Women's Literature* (Spring, 1993).

For information on Janet Little, I am indebted to the director of the Kyle and Carrick District Library and Museum Services, Ayr, Scotland.

A grant from the Huntington Library, San Marino, California, made the consultation of texts and much of this research possible. I thank the many staff members at the library who facilitated my research. At my home institution, the interlibrary loan and circulation offices in Love Library were very helpful.

For valuable answers to queries, I thank Elaine Hobby, Elizabeth Kowaleski-Wallace, Joanna Lipking, and Mitzi Myers; I thank Donna Landry for a fine reading of the manuscript. For general assistance, I thank research and work-study students Kate Flaherty, Michelle Miller, Nicolle French, and Jennifer Putzi. Warm thanks to Roma Rector and Angela Volzke for typing the manuscript so carefully and to Thomas Bestul and Robert Haller for advice about difficult script; additionally, I am indebted to Robert Stock for a useful consultation on *The Messiah* and Robert Haller for an illuminating discussion of "Wise Sentences."

CHAPTER TWO

Mary Collier: Women's Labor, Gender/Class Identity, and Nation Building

In the midst of a shifting English philosophy of labor, nationalism, and economic order, washerwoman Mary Collier from Hampshire wrote about insupportable social conditions and male attitudes in *The Woman's Labour* (1739), a pastoral with a difference.[1] Twenty-three years later, she published another slim but equally arresting volume of poems.[2] Coming on the feminist scene several decades after Sarah Fyge, Mary Astell, and Lady Mary Chudleigh, Collier introduced a new dimension to advocacy texts.[3] After the feminist protests of the 1690s, headlined by Astell's strong polemics, few had followed. Delarivière Manley and Eliza Haywood toned down their protests while Catherine Trotter and like-minded women penned occasional challenges until the 1720s.[4] But by and large, a near silence reigned from the 1720s until the 1730s.[5] By 1739, when *The Woman's Labour* appeared, other feminist texts—three in particular—displayed the resentment that persisted about the state of female education, lack of access to employment, and the life of married women: first, Lady Mary Wortley Montagu penned a vigorous protest;[6] second, the pseudonymous "Sophia" argued for the superiority of women;[7] and third, an anonymous reviewer in *The Gentleman's Magazine* decried male usurpation of female jobs.[8] With the licensing laws changed, profit-motivated publishers now recognized their vested interest in repromoting controversy around women as the political infighting which characterized Walpole's administration began to wane.[9]

With *The Woman's Labour*, Mary Collier initiates a tradition of working women's poetry. Included in every edition of Collier's vol-

umes, the poem was written in response to a popular poem by
Stephen Duck entitled *The Thresher's Labour* that was published in
1730.[10] In the autobiographical preface to the expanded 1762 edition
of *The Woman's Labour*, Collier describes how Duck's poem infuriated her in its relegation of female field-workers to the status of dil-
atory, feckless characters. Her decision to respond was prompted by
the encouragement of a family who had temporarily employed her.
Thus her text, she warns us from the outset, is a mediated one:

> After several Years thus Spent, [in Petersfield, washing and
> brewing], Duck's Poems came abroad, which I soon got by
> heart, fancying he had been too Severe on the Female Sex in his
> Thresher's Labour brought me to a Strong propensity to call an
> Army of Amazons to vindicate the injured Sex: Therefore I
> answer'd him to please my own humour, little thinking to make
> it Public. It lay by me several Years and by now and then
> repeating a few lines to amuse myself and entertain my com-
> pany it got Air.[11]

Not coincidentally, these poems by Stephen Duck and Mary
Collier reflect, and emerge during, economic instability. The fracture
of English country life caused by the enclosure of land and the entry
of Britain on the world stage partly explain Duck's account of laborers' physical and psychological hardship.[12] Enclosures, besides, cut
down on their access to common land. Nor could laborers easily
migrate from southern counties like Wiltshire and Hampshire since
no large industrial towns in the vicinity offered better opportunities
and guaranteed employment.[13] The county of Wiltshire, where Duck
worked, was probably enclosed somewhat later than Hampshire,
where Collier labored: "The swathe running from the southern counties up through the Central and East Midlands to Lincolnshire and
the East Riding of Yorkshire," which included Wiltshire and
adjoined Hampshire, was still open land in the early eighteenth century. The sixty-four acts that had been passed between 1740 and
1749 to enclose that crescent of land had swelled to about four hundred by the end of the century.[14] These poets were accordingly
responding to a complex transitional situation which disrupted jobs
and laborers' lives; they were explicating a nation-in-motion, an
evolving scene.

Rural English society was separating along class lines into land-
lords, leaseholding farmers, and landless laborers: "The result was
the transfer from the village community to the individual farmer of
a whole range of economic decisions which had hitherto been decided

collectively."[15] As workers, both Duck and Collier had experienced personal and class inequality. Consequently, their poems doubled as unstated laments for the destruction of traditional community control, for legally enacted territorial and social transformations that brought the rural laboring class into a new public focus.

Not surprisingly, laborers like Duck and Collier rarely emerged as published writers. With limited access to publication and rare encouragement to protest despite the popularity of printing, rural laborers in England had scant opportunity to publicize their views on any matter, let alone on this difficult situation. If they ignored the odds and wrote nonetheless, they needed patrons to help them publish; otherwise they would be guaranteed "to blush unseen / And waste their sweetness on the desert air." The last few years of Sir Robert Walpole's influence on national culture particularly accentuated this problem. While encouraging writers who advanced his political agenda, Walpole forced many among them into politics or toward booksellers who proffered financial blandishments.[16] In a sense, Duck and Collier were lucky to find patrons—in Collier's case, her employers. Since the reading public was skeptical about the authenticity of writer-laborers, class superiors often promoted the cause of the authors in the prefatory apparatus. In Mary Collier's case, the editions of *The Women's Labour* that appeared in 1739 and 1740 diverge most of all in their prefatory apparatus. But first I want to revert to the poem itself in which Collier discusses experiences of female field-workers as well as her life as a washerwoman.

Opening *The Woman's Labour* with an ironic apostrophe to Duck, Collier wasted no time in denouncing the lot of women. Several times she returns to the double shift endured by women who labored in the fields and at home, and their unremitting lack of rest:

> Immortal Bard! thou Fav'rite of the Nine!
> Enrich'd by Peers, advanc'd by CAROLINE!
> Deign to look down on One that's poor and low,
> Remembring you yourself was lately so;
> Accept these Lines: Alas! what can you have
> From her, who ever was, and's still a Slave?
> No Learning ever was bestow'd on me;
> My Life was always spent in Drudgery:
> And not alone; alas! with Grief I find,
> It is the Portion of poor Woman-kind.[17]

Collier represents herself self-effacingly in the first person while extravagantly elevating Duck to immortal ranks; her quietly embedded envy logically complements her sentiments. Regretting that she appears giftless before him, she images herself as a lowly and ill-esteemed individual. References to personal events underscore the autobiographical dimension, perhaps to assure readers of the account's authenticity. Speaking with a collective voice, she accentuates that her plight affects all women: "It is the Portion of poor Woman-kind." Praising Duck, assuming no airs, and stressing her industry, she indirectly claims the cultural respect tendered to her laboring, male counterpart.

The second section confirms the suspected mockery of Duck in the opening apostrophe. With a mythological reference to Danae, sweet-tongued poets, and the golden age now past when women were treated worshipfully, now she bemoans: "We are the objects of your Scorn at last." Mocking the fact that Duck compares his tasks to those of Hercules, she chides him because he "let our hapless Sex in Silence lie / Forgotten, and in dark Oblivion die." She especially resents his cavalier remarks about haymaking, a task frequently performed by females as well as males.[18] Contesting his charge that women laze around, she sarcastically enquires if he finds stopping to eat a waste of time. A proud Collier announces that conversation, including gossip, constitutes a special pleasure for women—perhaps (she hints) because they have something worth saying. The gossip that Duck disparages perpetuates—in Collier's view—communal values, and just as much to the point, an opportunity for art.[19]

Collier further negotiates the question of gender: on the one hand, the honest farmer who employs female haymakers is sensitive to female industry; on the other, husbands callously take extensive female responsibilities for granted. This scenario nullifies Duck's contempt for the bullying farmer who hires foolish women. Homely details emphasize her point and her veracity: husbands ignore post-prandial conversation as well as tearful infants during self-ordained (patriarchal understood) sleeping hours; the exacting demands of a parsimonious mistress in wintertime means too little soap for washing and not enough fire for warmth; women are by no means automatically supportive of other women when class authority and profit are at stake.

The third section cajoles sympathy from the reader with a list of matter-of-fact obligatory chores that underscores a nationwide work ethic, commencing at sundown after fieldwork: a laboring woman typically tidies the house, cooks, feeds swine, makes beds, welcomes the spouse home, mends clothes, feeds children. The next day the cycle resumes. At work in the fields, despite carrying fractious children around, women labor on a par with men. Even so,

"Had we ten hands, we could employ them all . . . We have hardly ever *Time to dream*" (p. 11).

Thus Collier energetically endorses women's equality as laborers in the field and washerwomen in others' houses while describing the work at home that additionally burdens women. She underscores the excessive work demanded from females at the hands of thoughtless husbands. She expects more humane treatment from her employers. She may be a lowly washerwomen from Petersfield in Hampshire who has not been, like Stephen Duck, "advanced by [Queen] Caroline" (p. 1). Nonetheless, she is not working for a "Turk" who expects silence (p. 8). Instead, she is laboring rural English womanhood personified, working with peas and corn during the harvest season, boiling bacon and dumplings at night all year round, and charring in the winter, the last job made more demanding due to the delicacy of fashionable fabric imported from Holland and India. A mug of hearty British ale is one of her few comforts in the cold months. Her rights may be constrained but she is an Englishwoman, entitled to be treated with common decency. Obliquely then, she calls for a national identity that recognizes the right to fair treatment and gender equality. To dissipate the idea that men work harder than women, she dramatizes the difficulty of charring during inclement winter months, describing how she was forced to clean brass and iron so vigorously that blood ran from her hands. She compares her situation to that of the soiled workers described by Duck:

Colour'd with Dirt and Filth [after cleaning dishes]
   we now appear;
Your threshing *sooty Peas* will not come near.
All the Perfections Woman once could boast,
Are quite obscur'd and altogether lost. (P. 16)

Before sunrise she washes the delicate linen garments of her mistress, again till the blood runs; such exacting industry elicits only sixpence or eightpence. A bitter couplet encapsulates her feelings: "For all our Pains, no Prospect can we see / Attend us but *Old Age* and *Poverty*" (p. 15).

Work under this mean-spirited martinet of a mistress involves not only constant washing but also cleaning huge amounts of pewter: "Brought in to make compleat our Slavery" (p. 15). For married and unmarried women workers alike, work never stops. Despite minimal hours allotted for sleep, the mistress sometimes rouses workers at midnight to start brewing.[20] At other times they are expected to work round the clock without sleep. Appealing to readers' compassion, Collier compares Duck's lot to that of Sisyphus, while women's work resembles that of Danaus's daughters who must ceaselessly fill bottomless tubs. Laboring women strive as "industrious Bees do hourly strive / To bring their Loads of Honey to the Hive" (p. 17). The unvarying iambic pentameters reinforce the endlessly repetitive labor, which "increases as the Year goes round."[21]

The abrupt conclusion to the poem punctuates the hard lot of working women at the hands of their employers: "Their sordid Owners always reap the Gains / And poorly recompense their Toil and Pains."[22] Its jolt reproduces the interrupted nature of laboring women's lives, particularly those who toiled seasonally in the country and others who were hired by the hour, both in large houses and in the fields.[23] The sudden stop emblematizes the lack of security, her poignant recognition that no positive, material recompense awaits her, only dire straits. In her own words: *"Old Age* and *Poverty"* (p. 15).

To contextualize the poem for a readership who doubt a washerwoman's cultural capacities, the first edition by "Mary Collier, now a Washer-woman, at Petersfield in Hampshire" contains a short preface by M. B., who affirms the poet's authenticity and pleads for goodheartedness to be extended toward Collier in her effort to earn a few extra pounds. The fact that she still works as a washerwoman in her old age emphasizes the seasonal, unpredictable job market.[24] According to Dorothy M. George, "among the longest hours of outworkers [in London] were those of the wretched women who went out to wash by the day."[25] Signing herself both a patron and apologist, M. B. mentions twice in the 230-word preface that washing clothes is a "tedious," "tiresome" occupation. But she also advises that if laundresses read the poem, less gossip and family disruption would ensue, an indirect affirmation of Duck's accusation of female loquacity.[26] Perhaps condescendingly, perhaps compassionately, she applauds the author's industry, humility, and unusual talent, "something considerably beyond the common Capacity of those of her own Rank and Occupation."[27] M. B. radiates an almost proprietorial pride in Collier's abilities.

Additionally, the third printing of the first edition boasts a number of male signatories who were clearly proud of Petersfield. Their collective statement is as follows: "We, whose names are hereunto subscribed, being Inhabitants of the Borough of Petersfield, in the County of Southampton, do hereby certify, that we know Mary Collier, the Washerwoman of Petersfield, and that she is the real Author of an epistle to Stephen Duck, called the Woman's Labour;

and also of (a paraphrase on the third and fourth Chapters of Esdras, called) the Three Wise Sentences, therewith published.[28] Signed by us at Petersfield, September 21st, 1739." The signatures attached are: "A. Matthew John Clement, Esq., Edward Rookes, Esq., John Shackleford, Esq., Charles Eades, Thomas Swannack, Thomas Stillwell, W. Clement, Thomas Bradly, Thomas Peace."[29]

Such eminent male authority, including three esquires, privileges Petersfield as well as Mary Collier while, in their need to authenticate Collier at all, underscoring her marginality. Since Stephen Duck had male patrons early on who read his work, his authenticity was never questioned; the Earl of Macclesfield read Duck's poems to the queen as early as 1730.[30] These men collectively recognize that is is harder to believe a *woman* laborer wrote verse. One of the signatories in question was Thomas Swannack, the same one recorded in *The History of Churcher's College, Petersfield* who witnessed an indenture on the 7 September 1731, which certified certain people as trustees of the land on which the College was to be built.[31] Though these witnesses would have been accepted locally, Swannack's public witnessing confirms the list of names as genuine as well as prestigious. By imbricating middle-class support, Collier suggests a strong local pride that is part of a larger national cultural identity. The most famous laboring-class female poet in England comes from Petersfield. Her rebuttal of the famous Duck is sold in the pamphlet shops near the Royal Exchange in London.

Moreover, this collective testimony appears when the enclosure of common land was destabilizing English country life. Their confirmation statement would have underscored some cross-class cultural stability and unity. Paradoxically, while strenghthening country rivalries, their witnessing affirmed a new gendered contribution from the laboring class. As Duck's royal favor attracted numerous imitators, regional differentiation became constitutive of the evolving national identity: "The perpetual flash checking of credentials' eligibility [cultural superiority] becomes the prototype of social activity at all levels."[32]

In 1762 a revised edition of *The Woman's Labour* appeared with new poems that also addressed working women's poetry and marriage.[33] Mary Collier seems to have been about seventy-two years old at the time.[34]

The prefatory material to the later edition includes Collier's autobiographical preface, "Some Remarks of the Author's Life drawn by herself," that newly contextualizes all previous poems. The fact that Mary Collier now writes her own prefatory apparatus and includes important information about herself marks a new confidence, a keener sense of her cultural location, and her rights as an individual. She now feels socially validated and a mini-memoir is her testimony. She was born—she states—"near Midhurst in Sussex of poor, but honest Parents." Educated by her mother, she was sent out to labor when her mother died, "as the Country afforded." She continued to live with her father till his death, after which she came to Petersfield, where she washed and brewed "and such labour." When she read Stephen Duck's poems, she deemed him "too severe on the Female Sex" and felt like marshaling "an Army of Amazons to vindicate the Female Sex." Answering him privately for personal satisfaction, she subsequently read the poems aloud for the amusement of local company for a few years. The spouse of a sick gentlewoman whom she tended transcribed *The Woman's Labour* and circulated the poem against Collier's wishes. As a result, many people advised her to have it printed. "I comply'd to have it done at my own charge, I lost nothing neither did I gain much, others ran away with the profit" (p. ix). Then a gentleman invited her to write a poem, "The Happy Husband," which she now "consigns" to the reader "and your Generosity to use as you please." She continued in Petersfield as a washerwoman till she was sixty-three, then managed a farmhouse near Alton till she was seventy and incapacitated, when she retired.

The circumstances that produced Collier's later text are finely spelled out; she is no longer a humble neophyte unable or unprepared to speak for herself. At the same time, she must (we suspect) remain unassuming to please her employers. The third-person reference to herself as author unsettles her humble self-representation. She also voices laboring Englishwomen committed to the double shift. By listing books she has read, which include "Speed and Bakers Chronicles, Fox's Acts and Monuments of the Church, [and] Josephus," she validates her intellectual and spiritual endeavors while underscoring her Protestant orientation.

The title to the first new poem is a case in point: "An Epistolary Answer to an Exciseman, Who doubted her being the Author of the *Washerwoman's Labour*." Reminding the exciseman that accused people have the right to a hearing, she remains polite and matter-of-fact: "Good Sir, By our English Laws / The Accused Party may / Have leave to plead, themselves to clear, / But you condemn Straightway" (p. 30). Then she quietly exposes his rudeness and jeers because he passed sentence without conducting an investigation; he is not "infallible, nor fit / To fill the Papal Chair." Only "poor, despised I" know who wrote the book; this assertion of authorship contradicts her self-canceling posture. She also upbraids him for his snobbish, skeptical, boorish attitudes:

> Tho' my Extraction was so low,
>   And I to labour bred;
> Yet Stories of the Pagan Gods,
>   I oft have seen, and read.
>
> And were you now in Petersfield
>   Or I in Gloucestershire;
> What you have Judg'd impossible,
>   I wou'd plainly make appear.
>
> But why shou'd you our Sex condemn;
>   And Women all despise
> We never with you interfere,
>   Nor trouble the Excise. (P. 31)

The same uncluttered dialogue informs the conversation-poem between "The Happy Husband and the Old Bachelor." The husband is a country gentleman happily married to a "sober virtuous wife." Out for a stroll, he chances upon his neighbor, also a gentleman with "a rural seat, which for long Space / Had gone in the Paternal race," a dual reference to his bachelor status and the exclusion of females from inheritance. While enjoying wine and ale at the bachelor's home, the married gentleman is baited by his host for wishing to return home. The husband cheerfully replies to the bachelor's boast of an unrestricted life.

> I never did repent my choice,
> I wou'd not have the Golden Chain,
> Of Hymen be unlink'd again.
> Nor wou'd I leave my Dearest Wife,
> To gain the greatest good of life; . . .
> While you abroad unsettled roam
> For want of such a Spouse at home;
> Tis an unhappy life you lead. (Pp. 34–35)

The bachelor gleefully informs the scandalized gentleman that he "may have Sons and Daughters too, / Without the trouble of a Wife / . . . Your counsel doth not please my mind, / Because I hate to be con-fin'd." Pursuing the debate on sexual politics, the husband replies that women would be "virtuous, just and kind" if more spouses

behaved civilly. Instructed by his happy neighbor, the bachelor
finally repents:

> My loving friend, I plainly See
> Good counsel you have given me. . . .
> I hope I shall reform at last.
> But first my care shall be apply'd
> To chose a virtuous loving Bride, . . .
> So may we find our Joys increase,
> For Virtue's ways are paths of peace. (P. 40)

Collier has treated the reader to a carefully orchestrated dialogue-
in-verse on the advantages of marriage for men, or so it seems. Perhaps she jabs sarcastically since she is quietly silent about the advantage of marriage for women. But at a slant, she has aired the sexually
biased law of primogeniture, as well as general and legal discrimination against women.[35] The buried text publicizing the unmarried Collier's avoidance of this trap resonates with a trace of self-congratu-
lation. Moreover, a poem named "A Gentlemen's Request to the
Author on Reading the Happy Husband and the Old Bachelor"
includes "Her [Collier's / the narrator's] Answer." The gentleman
requests the speaker to explain why single *women* should not marry.
She defends her status with an attack on patriarchal mores, accentuated in the bite of the final "freedom":[36]

> Most Men are now so viciously inclin'd
> That happy Wives are very hard to find;
> And as for discontented Maids I own,
> Any Such persons are to me unknown, . . .
> So Rev'rend Sir, I hope you will excuse
> The ignorance, and freedom of the Muse. (P. 41)

Collectively, Collier's new poems in the 1762 edition of *The
Woman's Labour* attest to a conflicted life. The presence of multiple
interlocutors in a series of sprightly conversations enables her to
ventriloquize variant perspectives. Particularly, she displays the
quality of life that laboring females endure, as well as married and
single women of any class.[35]

Poems of Mary Collier . . . A New Edition overlaps to some
extent with the revised 1762 edition of *The Woman's Labour* just discussed, yet important differences obtain. Once again, the publisher
includes *The Woman's Labour*, now the source of Collier's fame.

The first new poem in *A New Edition* derives from Scripture and functions as a counterpart to the "Three Wise Sentences" included in the 1739 edition. Signifying the strength and importance of Protestantism in terms of defining the nation, the Bible is synonymous with cultural safety. The contemporary celebrity of George Frederick Handel is a case in point. In the anthem that Handel wrote for George II's coronation in 1727, he described prophets who anointed the king. In the oratorios, he elaborated on the idea of Israel (i.e., Britain) rescued courageously by spiritual leaders: "a violent and uncertain past was to be redeemed by the new stoutly Protestant Hanoverian dynasty."[38] On a related note, Collier's "Wise Sentences" signifies the rebuilding of Jersualem (Britain), thanks to the persistent and brave Zorobabel. From *A New Edition,* "The First and Second Chapters of the First Book of Samuel Versified" expands or reformulates that thematic to include the issue of gender. Collier's adaptation narrates the tale of Hannah's frustration when she could neither bear a child nor silence her rival wife, the jealous though fertile Peninnah. But wise Hannah knows that God's will spurs her life; that if she has children, they will be God's gift. When Samuel is born, she honorably keeps her word and he is subsequently called on to execute God's plan. As in *The Woman's Labour,* Collier applauds the work of women. Despite understandable temptations to be angry, Hannah nurtures an inner knowledge of future triumph. And her containment and patience, in the end, serve her well. This woman's labor has a different but equally special significance. Hannah's ability to "labor" may be challenged, but she persists and never surrenders, a worker in the (re)productive field of female endeavor.

As the worthy leader of the nation to whom she gives birth, Samuel complements Hannah's own worth. To press the parallels a little further, perhaps Collier indirectly is applauding her personal resolve, while underscoring that of others. Hannah "produces" Samuel as Collier produces verses.[39]

A second poem in *A New Edition,* versifying and paraphrasing *Spectator* (vol. 5, no. 375), addresses similar issues in a diverse context. It chronicles the predicament of a young woman, Amanda, who refuses to become the mistress of a financially secure suitor, an act that would save her family from financial ruin. The poem foregrounds the morality and wisdom of these formerly rich people who are now scraping by: "From good esteem, reduc'd to low degree . . . / Heaven forbid that we so vile shou'd be / By sin and shame to shift off poverty!" (pp. 51, 53). By the end, the wily suitor, now a reformed rake, restores the parents to their original wealth and marries

Amanda. The unreality of this transformation highlights the vulnerability of women in economic straits. In a neat binary confirmation,
the poem condemns male abuse of women while extolling sin-free
poverty, filial obedience, and marriage. Collier tips her hat, as it
were, to conventional morality and the importance of kinship while
spotlighting women's disadvantages. The poem reads like *The
Woman's Labour*, but sounds a different, more domestic note.

In "Elegy upon Stephen Duck" Collier pays tribute to her class
peer, dead by his own hand. She uses the sad occasion to point out
the differential in their situations. She observes that public reception of her poems was slight compared to Duck's. Duck was given a
small house and various minor court appointments by the Queen; he
became a yeoman of the guard, then a keeper of the Queen's Library,
and eventually took holy orders, retiring to the living of Byfleet, Sur-
rey, in 1752.[40] Meanwhile, Collier appears to have lived a relatively
conventional washerwoman's life, despite her small cultural success.

Twenty years of scrubbing paralleled Duck's uneven but mate-
rially comfortable career. So she chides him—somewhat unfairly—
for his self-advancement, as if the gender bias were a personal
rather than a political result. Nonetheless, she grieves him. His suicide accentuates Collier's sense of class solidarity that inflects the
end of *The Woman's Labour*, where workers are "industrious" drones
at the beck and call of "sordid owners."

The elegy opens with a moving apostrophe that sharply contrasts with the ironic address to Duck at the opening of *The Woman's
Labour*:

That wond'rous man in whom alone did join
A thresher, poet, courtier, and divine. . . .
The ornament, and grace of poverty.[41]

Lauding Duck for his spectacular rise, allying herself emotionally
with the thresher poet whose death will eclipse the sun's rays, she
sadly notes how adversely fame affected his life. Despite the "stain"
of his death, she grieves that he lost "inward peace of mind" which
"seldom dwells among the rich, or great." Her lamentation suggests
that she has shared something of Duck's dark nights of the soul; a
laborer's hard life is something she knows. This alliance of Collier
with Duck allows her text to help redefine cultural parameters.
England should have room for both of them, and more. In that
respect, she signs the limitation of national culture. She reconfirms
the values of *The Woman's Labour* while extolling Duck as a patriot,
unable to withstand the pressures of his prominent cultural status.

Aside from issues of gender and class, some of Collier's text reflects diversely on the process of building a nation. This thematic, however, is much more obliquely rendered, as if Collier were "reflecting" her cultural and political milieu rather than directly addressing the launching of British nationalism. According to Gerald Newman, the crucial years in that launching were the 1740s to the 1780s. Naval supremacy, the alliance with Frederic, military exploits in Canada and the Caribbean were the talk of the day. Mary Collier's poems span the first half of this momentous transition that included "the intensified sense of togetherness and collective destiny brought on by the Seven Years War. . . . The 'chronic' sense of military, economic and diplomatic competition with France . . . the well-justified sense of alien cultural invasion." By the 1750s," Newman continues, "the theme of cultural protest was becoming more generalized, frantically hypochrondriac, and strident."[42] Since Roman Catholicism was anathema to the majority of Britons, gallophobia fostered this nationalist sentiment.

Collier's three principal poems that directly and indirectly address nation building are "Wise Sentences," "An Elegy to Norbert Powlett," and her poem to George III.[43] The first appears in the first edition of *The Women's Labour* and all subsequent editions in 1739 and 1740. Its title "The Three Wise Sentences from the First Book of Esdras, Chapters 3 and 4," derives from Esdras, an apocryphal book of the Bible; the "Wise Sentences" are aphorisms or "statements of significant import" that solve riddles. Tied in with clever resolutions and playful premises, the linked "sentences" add up to a narrative.

"Wise Sentences" tells the story of Darius, king of the Persians, and three youthful bodyguards who decide, after a royal banquet, to make a wager. Each young man will choose what he thinks is the most powerful force in the world; the king will determine the winner.[44] They leave their choices in notes for the king under his pillow. The first two men choose wine and the king, respectively, as the most powerful. The third bodyguard, Zorobabel, chooses women—"Women do bear away the Victory / From all on Earth"—and then truth (p. 19).

King Darius commands the young men to read the wise statements about their choices aloud. The first man contends that after drunken arguments, each participant returns to "the state he was before" (p. 21). The second contends that the king is strongest because "All Men on Earth submissively obey" (p. 22). They will die for the king in "foreign lands" or bring home the "choicest spoils."

In identifying the king as the principal source of strength, the second guard projects a promonarchic, proconquest, and patriotic argument. At one level, the answer is a compliment to George II, per-

haps Collier's own bid for preferment and patronage. Yet since the
king is the wrong answer, Collier could be intimating some of her
reservations about George II; perhaps she wants to inscribe a brief
oblique commentary concerning somewhat coerced loyalty toward
the monarch by workers like Duck and Collier herself. In using the
apocrypha, she questions, even undermines, the appropriateness of
unexamined obedience:

> How strong then is the *King*, whose regal Sway
> All Men on Earth submissively obey!
> They yield Obedience to his princely Will,
> And ready are his Pleasure to fulfil: . . .
> While those whose Bus'ness is to Till the Ground,
> With whom a Sword or Spear is seldom found,
> Manure their Land, their fruitful Vineyards dress; . . .
> And when the Harvest doth their Toil reward,
> They bring the Tribute to their *Sovereign Lord*.
> If any hapless Wretch the *King* displease,
> His Neighbours ne'er dispute, but on his seize;
> If he bid spare, they spare; if he bid kill,
> They ready are his Pleasure to fulfil. (Pp. 22–23)

Zorobabel is the third and most noble contestant, "a royal
Youth of David's kingly Race" who speaks his "Mind and Writing" (p.
24). He first makes a long argument in favor of women's "mortal
strength" (p. 27). He argues that women bear the world through
childbirth: "They nourish those that plant the fruitful vine" and
clothe people. Men cannot be content "Unless they can a *women's*
favor gain" (p. 24); a man would abandon everyone for a loving and
pure woman and work for money to please her (p. 26). In the midst
of these explanations about the lengths to which men will go for love
of women, several lines describe Darius's power and the obedience
that he commands. But Zorobabel goes on to mention that he
recently saw the "fair Apame" playfully remove Darius's crown and
strike him in jest, despite the fact that "his power is such / 'Tis Death
to strike, no less than Death to touch" (p. 26). Some men who loved
women, the text continues, were "reduc'd to utmost misery."
    At this point, Zorobabel's behavior diverges from the version
told in Esdras. Instead of conflating women and truth as principal
strengths, he declares that women alone constitute moral strength.
In the contention that women create leaders, "Wise Sentences" echoes "First Samuel" with its endorsement of Hannah's worthiness.
Notably, Collier chooses the tale of Esdras, wherein the young body-

guard who understands the worth of women is rewarded and becomes a national hero. Positive male leaders—she hints indirectly in several poems—estimate women appropriately. But Zorobabel, shortly afterwards, supplements and even transcends his choice of women by favoring truth (God) as the paramount power; unlike the other contestants, he chooses twice and prioritizes his choices: "Strong is the Truth, who did create all things [including strong women] . . . Almighty Truth, which ever shall endure" (p. 28). In other words, the strength of Truth or God incorporates the strength of women and hence is greater.

But the point about women's moral strength still stands. Biblical exegeticist Jacob Myers alters this reading of 1 Esdras to one that privileges women:

Zerubbabel began his observation by agreeing that wine and the king were indeed powerful. Nevertheless women were even more powerful since they were the mothers of kings and the bearers of those who plant and cultivate vineyards 'from which comes wine.' Nor is that all. Women make men's clothes and give them reputation. Consider the fact that though men are enamored of gold and silver or any other desirable thing, they will drop them at once upon sight of a charming woman. Do not men leave their parents and even their native land to cling to a wife? Actually women, however unobtrusively, dominate men who slave and labor to support them. Men endure the deprivations of war, the danger of wild beasts, and will even steal for their wives. Indeed men have been known to take leave of their senses over women. There is a host of examples of prominent women in the Bible—Sarah, Rebekah, Deborah, Naomi and Ruth, Esther, Judith, etc. . . . Women were no less influential among the Persians as the Apame episode illustrates. They were often impressed by women.[45]

Certainly "truth" is ultimately privileged, but it is centered in the context of female worthiness. Furthermore, a note on nation subtly inscribes itself after the extraordinary (regicidal?) comment, intended to buttress the victory of God / Truth, that "kings are wicked, all wise men agree" (p. 29). Thus Darius is subsequently dethroned, in a sense: "In [Truth] alone is strength and Majesty (p. 29). Despite this, Darius responds to Zorobabel's argument with rewards galore—anything he requests—including kinship: he "commands that they his cousin should him call" (p. 30). Flattering Darius's vanity, Zorobabel asks for Jerusalem to be rebuilt, the Temple to be raised, and holy vessels (often a code word for women) restored. If he completes the project, "Immortal Honour Thy Reward will be" (p. 31). His logic appeals to the king, who orders the restitution of Jerusalem and waives tribute in perpetuity. The poem ends with Zorobabel's lavish praise of his "Creator" (p. 32). Hence, the third guard, Zorobabel, who goes beyond his praise of women in favor of God/Truth ends up wealthy and with permission to wear the royal purple. The king also grants his wish that Jerusalem be rebuilt—as the Hanoverian kings, *mutatis mutandis,* rebuild the reputation of Protestant England. She imagines a national community through "historical" eyes, "the invisible outline whose unquestioned boundaries could only be strengthened by the apparent fierceness of the battles fought in its name and on its ground."[46] Zorobabel is nobler than the others because "he did the living God adore" (p. 24). At first he commended women ardently, including King Darius's love, the coquettish Apame. Nothing can compare with women's moral strength, in Zorobabel's view, except for Almighty Truth that encompasses it. This statement accords with the evidence of *Woman's Labour;* it is a paraphrase that indirectly validates Collier's confrontation with Stephen Duck's argument about women in *The Thresher's Labour?* Collier complicates her national argument by inflecting it with identifications of gender and class.

After being rewarded for his patriotic desire to have Jerusalem reconstructed, Zorobabel replies to the sovereign:

> When first thou didst the *Persian* Sceptre wield,
> That thou the peerless City wouldst rebuild;
> That glorious Temple, which was once the praise
> Of all the Earth, thou vow'dst again to raise; . . .
> No other Thing, great Prince! do I require. . . . (P. 31)

On a related note, King Darius's reign makes this cultural competition possible since he is patron of the arts. Here, Handel's championed parallels between Britain and Israel—despite his outsider status—also resonate. Like Handel, Collier applauds scriptural heroes who resemble contemporary heroes while simultaneously stressing Protestantism and its values. Perhaps a cross-class national trend functions here. Yet unlike Handel and other British patriots of the time, Collier genders the scriptural argument, her vantage point distinctly plural.[47]

The name of Zorobabel or Zeurbbel also lends a critical meaning to the tale.[48] A descendant of David, Zorobabel was appointed governor of Judah while the temple in Jerusalem was being rebuilt during the Babylonian exile. Then Zorobabel mysteriously vanishes from the narrative, with no explanation. Perhaps Collier aims to subtly mark what happens if an individual disrespects authority. On the other hand, popular contrasts between scriptural and eighteenth-century heroes would find echoes here. Zorobabel will help to save the new and intrepid Protestant Hanoverian dynasty from Britain's tumultuous, Catholic past.

Not until *A New Edition* appears in 1762 do readers learn that "Wise Sentences" was a poem *recommended* by employers. Since the poem upholds spiritual values and underscores the importance of women, it effectively affirms Collier's gynocentric vantage point, indicated in *The Women's Labour*. Concurrently, it applauds the honor of a conquering king and his honor in an era of intensifying British colonialism. "Wise Sentences" supports a nationalist first impulse that connects Collier's class and English identity.

The second poem that touches on nation building eulogizes a local burger; appearing in the *New Edition*, it is entitled "An Elegy on the much lamented death of Norton Powlett, Esquire; who departed this life at Petersfield, June the 4th, 1741." As Mary Collier composed the 1762 volume, Britain's global position was drastically transforming. "The world-wide conquests of 1758–60," in one historian's words, "can to some extent be regarded as the final triumph of the old Whig foreign policy."[49] The European architects of these victories and of British naval supremacy were William Pitt and King Frederic of Prussia, commonly regarded as Protestant champions in the Seven Years' War against the non-Protestant order of France, Austria, and Russia (1756–1763). Collier does not project Powlett as a national champion, but rather as a stalwart Englishman who stood his ground in fighting the corruption of "rotten Boroughs." From 1711 to 1741 he "bravely stood, Supporting justice, and his country's good." He is a local soldier or regional patriot who preserves Britain's reputation for justice. For thirty years Powlett championed several causes but notably lost the critical election to be a burgess. He met an untimely death while aiding the poor in his district: "His memory lives in ev'ry honest heart." (p. 49). Collier testifies to her compensatory grief: "the pensive muse at length attempts relief," ending with conventional "loud hallelujahs to his heav'nly king." Powlett's example should induce people to try "Once more to gain our ancient liberty!/ Rememb'ring still that noble Powlett's strife / To save our freedom, ended with his life!" (p. 50). Although a simple eulogy, the poem also repeats the message of "Wise Sentences" about intrepid lieges meting out justice abroad.

The panegyric to Powlett functions as a silent companion piece to Duck's elegy, two worthy men respected by their countrymen and women. In Powlett's case, local people pay tribute because he subscribed, without compromise, to "English" values about freedom and justice.

The third poem that touches on nation building doubles as a royal tribute. Mary Collier's final eulogy, "On the Marriage of George III; Wrote in the Seventy-second Year of Her Age" reconfirms her cultural legitimacy in establishment circles. Having praised the king for rescuing Britain from Roman Catholicism and its dictatorial teachers, she compliments fair Charlotte who joined George III "In the soft tie of Hymen's sacred bands . . . / May you to high and low a pattern be, of conjugal love and fidelity" (p. 58). Marked with a complex feminized identity, George III "adorns" the throne, a deserving recipient of such honor after a "blooming" youth in virtue's path. He affirms national pride.

Acknowledging Britain's alliance with Frederic the Great during the Seven Years' War, Collier praises the "lustre of the German blood" in the three Hanoverian Georges, intrepid leaders on a continuum with Zorobabel and Samuel. Royal Protestantism attracts Collier: "By heaven sent to save our native lands, / From popish slavery and tyrants hands" (p. 58). Wishing the monarchs a well-earned longevity, Collier displays King George and Queen Charlotte as a model for the rest of the nation: "many children's children live to see" (p. 58). Just as Zorobabel desires joy in eternity, so Collier wishes the same for George III.

But Collier's laudatory conclusion still inscribes some ambivalence: George III may be Britain's greatest patriot of all, but she does not hesitate to mark his "non-Englishness," or, put another way, his fortune in becoming part of a distinguished English, national scenario. In the three poems, Collier's overall commitment to the monarchs, to a local burgher, and to a heroic ancient king and his patriotic bodyguard radiates nationalist sentiment.

Mary Collier's poems comprise a sustained feminist manifesto of both famous and deprived, unrecognized people. She narrates an oppositional bucolic tale which yields traces of national pride. In attacking contemporary Stephen Duck and defending the labor and worth of women, Collier marshals a counterintuitive argument to the reigning sexual politics of the day. Decades before untutored genius ("uneducated poets") became a celebrated phenomenon, she signed herself as an individual who was proud to voice the unvoiced.

Adept at compromise—she had to be—Collier also cleverly scripts her own preservation by seeming to accommodate her employer's cultural choices. She lets their interventions speak for themselves, marking and highlighting her economic and social vulnerability. Clever dialogic interplay among diverse prefaces and advertisements further conveys the layers of mediation that she softly confronts, a knowledge of her own individual powerlessness, not explicitly spelled out until the 1760s. She exposes the reality of a working-class female condition in southern England and beyond its borders, an obvious patriot as well as a subaltern. In this age of expanding colonialism, moreover, Collier adds her reflections on Britain's global transformation. Yet that "national consciousness" does not seem to be—as women and class are—an integral (or conscious) part of her political agenda. Nonetheless , Collier's complex poems articulate and indirectly advance Britain's role abroad. Tracing still inchoate paths, she works persistently with ambivalences, with oblique conjecture about Britain's upcoming global prominence. Self-improvement emanates, through the act of writing and producing documents that narrate a suppressed tale. As a cultural agent, perhaps her principal source of power is exposure.

Through her poems, Mary Collier defines a new gendered and class identity that encompasses loyal working-class people who construct a vital culture that suggests the ongoing process of nation building and colonial incursions. In so doing, Collier also redefines the Anglo-Saxon national identity and circulates new formulations of Englishness.

CHAPTER THREE

Mary Scott: Historicizing Women, (En)Gendering Cultural History

By the 1750s, the switch from Mary Collier's early to late poems displays an evolving awareness about national identity, now conceptualized as distinctly Protestant and anti-French; upholding English liberties is paramount. After Collier's patriotic *New Edition* in the early 1760s and prior to the publication of Mary Scott's *The Female Advocate* in 1774, this nationalist sense was further spurred by the controversy over John Wilkes and his passionate identification with England.[1] Wilkes touted himself as the emblem of English freedom to the point where Samuel Johnson—a supporter of Wilkes—denounced patriotism as the last refuge of a scoundrel.

By 1774, the state of England aroused such controversy that Horace Walpole characterized it as corrupt, *tout court*.[2] At the same time, people like John Duncombe, who wrote *The Feminiad* (1754), were formulating new gendered definitions of Englishness and national culture.[3] In conjunction with the rising political activity of middle- and working-class people in the early 1760s, Mary Scott extended cultural boundaries by eulogizing middle-class Englishwomen.

In a 522-line poem entitled *The Female Advocate* (1774), Mary Scott consolidates the importance of gendered history by documenting the talents and accomplishments of fifty women from the sixteenth century on.[4] Her poem begins with Catherine Parr (1512–1548), Protestant author of *Lamentations of a Sinner* and King Henry VIII's last wife, and ends with the renowned contemporary Unitarian children's writer and educator, Anna Laetitia Aikin Barbauld (1743–1825). Among the remaining writers are sixteen titled women, twelve Bluestockings and women linked to Bluestocking circles. The rest hail almost exclusively from the middle class, vari-

27

ously designated as learned ladies, poets, linguists, essayists, translators, and devotional writers. All the women are English except for Constantia Grierson (c. 1704–1733), an Irishwoman who was also the only laboring-class writer.[5] Commenting on Grierson as a poet and the "perfect mistress of the *Hebrew, Greek, Latin,* and *French* languages; equally well acquainted with History, Divinity, Philosophy, and Mathematics,"[6] the narrator lauds Grierson's class and cultural transcendence in a deliberate evocation of Gray's *Elegy.* In this case, however, the poet is named and known in a gendered triumph.

Though her fortune low, her birth obscure, . . .
Sprung from a race illiterate, rude and poor;
To all th' emoluments of art unknown,
Yet Wit and Learning mark'd her
    for their own. (Pp. 15–16)

The Female Advocate establishes Mary Scott as the first woman to feature a historical lineage of accomplished women poets and prose writers who are a credit to England. Indirectly she argues for the education of women—how else can they refine their poetics? Scott silently constitutes herself as a member of that community.

Prior to the publication of *The Female Advocate,* commendatory poems and prose to women was mostly written by men; the Bible and classical texts supplied most of the examples. These tributes to learned women, also known as female worthies, had appeared sporadically.[7] Among them were Plutarch's *Mulierum Virtutes* (A.D. 95–100), Boccaccio's *De Claris Mulieribus* (c. 1359), and Chaucer's *Legend of Good Women* (1380–1386). These compilations mark the beginning of a documented female cultural heritage while works written by Western women themselves probably started with *La Cité des Dames* (c. 1405) by Christine de Pisan. The tradition developed by fits and starts.

After Thomas Heywood's *Gynakeion* (1624) and Charles Gerbier's *Elogium Heroinum* (1651), one of the earliest British female eulogists of women, Bathsua Makin, wrote *An Essay to Revive the Antient Education of Gentlewomen* in 1673. By charting the accomplishments of learned women over the centuries from Zenobia, Queen of Palmeria, to Constantia Sforza, Makin hoped to attract pupils to her London school. Gerbier similarly preferred the view that "woman is capable of as high improvement as man."[8] From Makin's list to Mary Scott's litany, tributes to women gradually came to constitute a cultural phenomenon.

Following the civil war and the bourgeois revolution in England, in which many women participated, the range of possibilities for praising women concomitantly widened in a middle-class parallel of Collier's polemic about laboring female conditions. A cult of origins, linked to nation building itself, was in the making; Englishwomen began to chronicle the accomplishment of their predecessors as part of a gendering of Hanoverian nationalism; they were intent on cultural separation from France, Spain, and Italy. By mid-eighteenth century, six men (but no women) published commendations to female worthies in as many years, evidence "of a sympathetic impulse felt mid-century toward creative and learned women."[9] The most important was George Ballard's *Memoirs* of "sixty more or less extended biographies" (1752), described by critic Myra Reynolds as "the first source of detailed and ordered, and in general, accurate information concerning the learned women of England."[10] Then came Theophilus Cibber's *Lives of the Poets* (1753). Scott seems principally indebted to those two eulogists and their collections of female poets, especially Ballard's historical approach in praising women from early times. After Cibber came John Duncombe's *The Feminiad. A Poem (1754)*, a "glorification of fifteen female geniuses." To give a whiff of contemporary sexual politics, Duncombe's poem slighted the texts of playwrights and scandal-memoirists as "dang'rous sallies of a wanton Muse."[11] Duncombe may also have collaborated with Cibber, since several writers included in the *Feminiad* appear in Cibber's *Lives*.

In 1755, George Colman and Bonnell Thornton edited *Poems by Eminent Ladies*, followed by Thomas Amory's two-volume *Memoirs of Several Ladies of Great Britain*, a "medley of unrelated observations, disquisitions, and opinions," and the anonymous *Biographium Femineum* (1766), which recorded "above fourscore British Ladies." Approximately speaking, of Scott's fifty female worthies, twenty appear in George Ballard's text and at least two—Mary Chandler and Anne Killigrew—come from that of Theophilus Cibber. From John Duncombe's list come Laetitia Pilkington and Hester Chapone, as well as Katherine Philips, who appears in all three lists. From George Colman's and Bonnell Thornton's *Eminent Ladies*, Scott may have independently selected Mary Barber, Mary Jones, and Mary Masters, although she probably knew of these contemporary writers, as well as some of the others.

After these midcentury paeans to middle-class English females, Mary Scott composed *The Female Adocate*, partly inspired by this male outburst of gynocentric commendation. She explains her motivation in the dedication, "To A Lady," indirectly stressing female national identity by underscoring their collective contribution to culture:

> Mr. Duncombe's Feminead you and I have often read with the most grateful pleasure; and undoubtedly you remember, that we have also regretted that it was only on a small number of Female Geniuses that Gentleman bestowed the wreath of Fame; and have wished to see those celebrated whom he omitted, as well as those who have obliged the world with their literary productions, since the publication of his elegant Poem. (P. v)

On the other hand, Scott also uses the preface to mark her dual aims. She upbraids the sentiments of "the generality (of men of sense and learning") whose opinions "are still very contracted" (p. vi).

She goes on to say:

> How much has been said, even by writers of distinguished reputation, of the distinction of sexes in souls, of the studies, and even of the virtues proper for women?: If they have allowed us to study the imitative arts, have they not prohibited us from cultivating an acquaintance with the sciences? Do they not regard the woman who suffers her faculties to rust in a state of listless indolence, with a more favourable eye, than her who engages in a dispassionate search after truth? And is not an implicit acquiescence in the dictates of their understandings, esteemed by them as the sole criterion of good sense in a woman? . . . But I flatter myself a time may come, when men will be as much ashamed to avow their narrow prejudices in regard to the abilities of our sex, as they are now fond to glory in them. (Pp. vi–vii)

With Duncombe's approach in mind, Mary Scott selected fifty women, embraced Duncombe's "feminiad" in a footnote, and omitted from her poem (except for one brief mention) the very six writers whom Duncombe had scolded for their "wanton muse": Aphra Behn, Susanna Centlivre, Delarivière Manley, Theresa Constantia Phillips, Frances Anne Hawes, Lady Vane, and Laetitia Pilkington. If the moral reputation of England is at stake, sullied writers should remain underground.

What specifically prompted a Somerset woman, living in relative obscurity, to locate herself in a mimetic relationship to a small, gendered cultural vanguard is partly answered by a look at her life.

Mary Scott was born about 1752 and lived for over two decades at Milborne Port in Somerset, West England, where her father was a linen merchant.[12] An obituary in *The Gentleman's Magazine* (1787) attests to her mother's "exemplary" life as an informal philanthropist.[13] Early in life, Mary Scott subscribed to evangelical doctrines, writing many hymns on the subject. The Scotts also had a son, Russell, who presided as the Unitarian minister at Portsmouth from 1788 to 1833.[14] By her own account, by the time she was fourteen Mary Scott had become ill, as well as religious, and creatively inclined. In "Rural Meditation" the speaker, seemingly very close to Scott herself, closes with quiet resignation: "Lord to thy sovereign will may I resign / And let me never from thy precepts fly."

By her twenty-first birthday, Mary Scott had entered a poem in the friendship book of her close friend, Mary Steele. Yet her health is so poor, she discloses, that she could scarcely pen her poems. Highlighting her affection for this poet-friend, she expresses desire for a permanent friendship. Scott continued to write these friendship poems—many unpublished before her death—for most of her life. One of the last poems states:

> O say when life's vain hopes, and fears are o'er,
> And this pale form in Death's dark shade shall sleep,
> Wilt thou my Exit with a Tear deplore
> And by my Urn one mournful vigil keep?[15]

Scott mysteriously implores Mary Steele to defend her memory "from each attack of slander's venom'd tongue"; perhaps she feared a negative response to *The Female Advocate*.

Both Scott's illness and her friendship with Mary Steele explain the *Advocate*'s inception. First, Scott states in the dedication that she lay very ill during the three years before she wrote the poem; possibly her invalidism facilitated the copious research she undertook for the poem, since mobility seems to have been difficult for Scott. Anna Seward's letters to Mary Scott yield much of the known information about Scott during this period.[16] Scott's rigorous self-education both delighted and alarmed her close friend, to whom Scott bemoaned her failing eyesight. In reply, Seward commiserated and expressed a wish that Scott's eyes would regain "their strength, and again permit the streams of wisdom and genius to flow in upon your mind from the pages of ancient and modern literature."[17] Anna Seward's emphasis on Scott's research into ancient and modern literature confirms a contemporary vogue concerning national origins as well as the promotion of female culture. Both gendered and class culture became inscribed within this expansive definition of national identity. Mary Scott was garnering a small reputation in her own community as an archivist and scholar, a restorer of national pride. By the 1780s, Mary Steele endorses her knowledge of science, a subject that crops up in *The Female Advocate*.

Second, Mary Scott became attracted to Unitarian ideas around this time. The year she wrote *The Female Advocate*, she was introduced to John Taylor when he was a student at Daventry Academy, a Unitarian establishment in Coventry, North England, administered by Dr. Caleb Ashworth. She probably met him when she took her Unitarian brother Russell to the academy to attend school.[18] Due to her strict concept of filial obedience, she refused to marry Taylor for fourteen years, until after her mother died. Not long before, Samuel Richardson and Hester Chapone had debated this issue of parental duty and obedience.[19]

Third, Scott's correspondence with Mary Steele reveals a wide circle of female friendship that existed in the English provinces. Mary Steele's aunt was Anne Steele, the famous Baptist religious writer, and a friend of Mary Scott. Together they founded an informal literary coterie that resembled seventeenth-century informal salons whose members had dubbed themselves by classical names.[20] The Somerset group did the same. Mary Scott was Myra, Mary Steele was Silvia, Anne Steele was Theodosia. Later, Mary Steele participated in the famous Leicester circle of women friends that included Elizabeth Heyrick, the famed abolitionist, and her friend and poet, Susanna Watts.[21] In their correspondence, Scott and Mary Steele avidly discuss their role and concerns as authors while lauding women writers, especially their beloved Anne Steele.

As individuals committed to a feminocentric culture, the Steele-Scott coterie members were self-conscious about their social role as writers and well aware of Bluestocking assemblies that had become the talk of London in 1774 when *The Female Advocate* was published.[22] Elizabeth Boscawen told the celebrated Mary Delany in 1770 that the *"female club* I told you of . . . meets . . . at certain rooms of Almacks . . . It is much the subject of conversation . . . The first fourteen who imagined and planned it settled its rules and constitutions . . . The ladies nominate and choose the gentlemen and vice versa."[23] Hannah More's popular poem *Bas Bleu* (1782) immortalized the activities of the Bluestocking salonières and "enraptured London Society."[24] Samuel Johnson called it a "very great performance."

The Bluestockings' commitment to gendered culture inspired women in the provinces and accentuated past concerns about female education from the seventeenth century on.[25] Education for women had also become a popular though controversial subject in the press. Such seventeenth-century polemicists on female education as Bathsua Makin and Mary Astell were followed by several early eighteenth-century writers, among them Viscountess Irwin, Lady Chudleigh, and Elizabeth Rowe. The Gentleman's Magazine complemented their efforts by applauding better treatment for women.[26]

This privileging of female intellectuality showed up intertextually in the culture at large. Sarah Robinson Scott—the sister of prominent Bluestocking Elizabeth Montagu, whose work was included in The Female Advocate—advocated female education in her novel, Millenium Hall (1762), that went into a third and fourth edition by 1767 and 1788.[27] A friend of Sarah Scott, Sarah Fielding argued similarly in The Female Governess. Fielding had also participated in Lady Miller's distinctive literary salon in Batheaston, just outside Bath.[28]

Female salons and commendatory verse, in addition to Scott's own scholarly pursuits, prompted The Female Advocate. But even so, Scott became reluctant to continue the poem: "Thinking myself unequal to the task, it was quickly laid aside, and probably never would have been resumed, had not your [her friend Mary Steele's] partiality to the Author led you to have been pleased with the specimen which you saw" (pp. v–vi). Ironically, Scott's name was omitted from nineteenth-century memoirs and from encyclopaedias and dictionaries of learned women.[29]

Female scholarship had begun to mark English culture. Scott's learned friends, her inclusion of Bluestocking texts, her extensive commentary on a range of texts from Catherine Parr and Catharine Macaulay to Constantia Grierson and Phillis Wheatley spotlight a cross-cultural historical tradition among women. Taking pains to sound the void of females, Scott refuses to countenance invisibility or content herself with sporadic mentions of female authors.

One corollary of Scott's emphasis on female scholarship is her self-representation not only as a poet, but as a scholar who supplemented her verse with copious footnotes; Scott participates in her own commentary about learned women.

First, the footnotes describing authors were half as long again as the five-hundred-word text and signified Scott's intention to write separate but complementary, parallel texts; these notes included not only biographies and bibliographies of differing lengths but textual sources and references to other texts. George Ballard's prodigious biographies may have served as Scott's model. This biographical cataloguing of learned women and their texts in itself constituted another polemic.

Put another way, *The Female Advocate* negotiates for an inclusive national identity in an England that had closed intellectual outlets to women.Scott braids gendered polemic, a commendatory text, and scholarly apparatus into a single text.

Scott opens *The Female Advocate* by acclaiming a cluster of sixteen virtuous, learned daughters of the Protestant Reformation— from the More, Coke, and Seymour sisters to Queen Catherine Parr, Lady Jane Grey, and Queen Elizabeth I. Scott's lineup, like Collier's, congratulates the new Hanoverian dynasty and contrasts its values with those of a corrupt Catholic past. Sketches of illustrious seventeenth-century women—the Duchess of Newcastle, Anne Killigrew, Katherine Philips, and Lady Rachel—trace a Protestant lineage through the Renaissance. Scott's reservation about the Duchess of Newcastle's inclination toward "fancy" affirms her commitment to "facts," even more sadly grotesque in light of her husband John Taylor's later condemnation of poetry after he joined the Society of Friends.[30]

Scott's continuum of queens and aristocratic women emphasizes cultural construction based on class while warding off any charge that she fails to represent women across class lines; her opinions about Catholics aside, Scott stakes a claim in recasting the English Protestant tradition.

But Scott's authorial choices also transcend the socially orthodox. After the sixteenth- and seventeenth-century roll calls, Scott glorifies Lady Mary Chudleigh's feminist views in *The Ladies Defence*; this poem attacked a 1699 wedding sermon by the Reverend John Sprint (entitled *The Bridewoman's Counsellor*) that supported wives' unconditional obedience toward husbands.

Most striking in the poem is Scott's foregrounding of relationships among personal friends and historical figures. Her encomium to Anne Steele is a notable case in point:

O yet may Heav'n its healing aid extend,
And yet to health restore my valued friend:
Long be it ere her gentle spirit rise,
To fill some glorious mansion in the skies. (P. 25)

Scott's esteem for Elizabeth Montagu's "Genius, Learning . . . [and] Worth" doubles as an implied compliment to the Bluestockings: she notes in the preface that "public favour has attested the merit of Mrs. Chapone's *Letters on the Improvement of the Mind*; and of Miss More's elegant *Pastoral Drama.*" Subsequently, Scott praises Montagu's "sweet Philanthropy" that validates her own vantage point: poets like herself were flouting prescribed rules for women in an age that underwrote separate spheres:

> O, sweet Philanthropy! thou guest divine!
> What permanent, what heart-felt joys are thine!
> Supremely blest the maid, whose generous soul
> Bends all-obedient to thy soft controul:
> Nature's vast theatre her eye surveys,
> Studious to trace Eternal Wisdom's ways;
> Marks what dependencies, what different ties,
> Throughout the spacious scale of beings rise;
> Sees Providence's oft-mysterious plan,
> Form'd to promote the general good of man.
> With noble warmth thence her expanded mind
> Feels for the welfare of all human-kind:
> Thence flows each lenient art that soothes distress,
> And thence the unremitting wish to bless! (P. 31)

Similarly Scott commended women on the borders of Bluestocking circles, Sarah Fielding and Catherine Talbot, as well as their contemporaries, Mary Barber, Mary Chandler, Mary Jones, Charlotte Lennox, and Lady Sarah Pennington. The fact that Lady Pennington's letters to her daughter had become a succès de scandale since she left her husband adds a more pointed political commentary about female marginalization to Scott's poem.[31] So does her inclusion of the learned Talbot's *Reflections on the Seven Days of the Week* (1770), and Constantia Grierson's poems that suggest Scott's debt to George Ballard.[32]

More unconventionally, when Scott pays tribute to Phillis Wheatley in her preface, she refashions national cultural identity along antislavery lines. By extolling the talent of Phillis Wheatley, who was sold in 1761 to a Boston family and visited Britain the summer before the publication of *The Female Advocate*, Scott refutes plantocratic contentions about black inferiority and quietly renegotiates the old debate about the humanity of African men and women.[33] She recasts traditional mythologies about Africans.[34] Furthermore, Scott's inclusion of Wheatley drew more attention to several widely publicized scandals concerning slaves, especially the famous trial of the slave James Somerset over his forced return to the West Indies. Defended by the famous abolitionist, Granville Sharp, and obliged to remain silent throughout the proceedings,

Somerset went to court and won his case in 1772. In another case where a slave had committed suicide rather than be sent back to the Caribbean, abolitionist Thomas Day had versified the narrative to much acclaim in 1773. Scott's appreciation for Phillis Wheatley also functioned as muted commentary on the bankruptcy of silencing slaves. Implicitly, she exposes widespread fear about black agency, whether spoken, written, or physical.

By affirming Phillis Wheatley, Scott identifies a positive national identity with abolitionist ideology. The Bluestockings themselves had been involved in Phillis Wheatley's visit while the press had lost no time in assailing her owners for hypocrisy. Britain should not, she insists as an abolitionist patriot, be a slave-holding country.

Scott's positioning of the historian Catharine Macaulay as one of the poem's centerpieces confirms Macaulay's commitment to freedom and justice as well as her keen sense of national identity: "A name to ev'ry son of freedom dear, / Which patriots yet unborn shall long revere" (p. 27).

The foregrounding of Macaulay also signs Scott's gendering of British culture in *The Female Advocate*. Macaulay emblematizes liberty and English principles. Countering an incomplete cultural tradition, she reconstructs a more representative one:

> O Liberty! Heav'n's noblest gift below,
> Without thee life were but one scene of woe:
> Beneath thy sway, in these auspicious isles,
> Science erects her laurell'd head, and smiles;
> Our great *Augustus* lives the friend of Arts,
> And reigns unrivall'd in their vot'ries Hearts. (P. 27)

From the beginning of the poem, Scott has stressed a gendered Protestant culture. Epitomizing this tradition, Macaulay links Scott's praise for women with solid efforts to redefine, even reconstitute national identity. Additionally, by highlighting Catharine Macaulay, Scott inscribes Whiggishness within her pantheon of values. Having recently published four volumes of *The History of England*, Macaulay marks herself as a cultural spokeswoman for the Whigs, inextricably associated with the principles of 1689, civil rights, limits on monarchical rule, and an egalitarian order. She had taken issue with Thomas Hobbes's propositions in an article published in 1767, and responded to Edmund Burke's pamphlet on "present discontents." Then she suggested solutions of her own. On a more social level (that might also explain Scott's attentiveness), she choreographed a lively political coterie in London in the early 1770s with which Scott may have been acquainted.[35] With her choices of Grierson, Wheatley, and Macaulay, Scott reconstructs a complex sociocultural history developed by women over the centuries that parallels that of men.

Underscoring her protestant eclecticism, Scott particularly honored "Miss Aikin" or Anna Laetitia Barbauld as she was known after her marriage, a prominent Unitarian writer. On a personal as well as a political note, John Taylor taught at Daventry Dissenting Academy, academic cousin to Warrington Dissenting Academy, where Barbauld was raised. That propinquity might have directed Scott's choice. She applauds Barbauld's "vivid intellectual paintings" and proceeds to a final meditation on female deprivation.

Having amply demonstrated female cultural worth, Scott denounces male expropriation of "the fair realms of knowledge" that denies intellectual pursuit to women:

> Supreme in science shall the Tyrant reign!
> When every talent all-indulgent Heav'n
> In lavish bounty to your share hath giv'n? . . .
> To them [women] see Genius her best gifts impart,
> And Science raise a throne in ev'ry heart!
> One turns the moral, one th' historic page;
> Another glows with all a *Shakespeare's* rage!
> With matchless *Newton* now one soars on high,
> Lost in the boundless wonders of the sky;
> Another now, of curious mind, reveals
> What treasures in her bowels Earth conceals. (P. 36)

Indeed, as Scott evinces in her warm debt to "The Female Right to Literature" by Canon Thomas Seward, father of Anna Seward, the female right to learning connects to patriotism and British global rule. After expatiating on the oppressed state of women in foreign lands, the speaker hails

> Happy Britain, dear parental land,
> Where Liberty maintains her latest stand!
> . . . Do Thy Sons, who claim
> A birth-right liberty, dispense the same
> In equal scale? why then does Custom bind
> In chains of ignorance the female mind?[36]

In other words, Britain cannot boast a positive, freedom-loving identity as long as women are denied access to knowledge. Scott's radical notion links political freedom and the right of females to education. By foregrounding Canon Seward's poem, she endorses his perspective on women. This fact is enhanced by the title page epigraph to *The Female Advocate* that comes from the canon's poem.

Scott's final diatribe inscribes a quiet personal note, since science fascinated her. Scott's friend Mary Steele testifies to this devotion in one of her poems. Deploring the exclusion of women from scientific pursuit and taboos against commending female accomplishments, Scott cleverly works this cultural counteropposition into her poem. The abrupt couplet complimenting some men for their "tributary lays" substantiates her case about women's raw treatment and mischievous exclusion. Scott relocates women in the cultural loop.

All in all, Scott adds the names of twenty-four women writers not contained in Ballard, Cibber, Duncombe, Colman, and Thornton.[37] They include Anna Laetitia Barbauld, Dorothea Mallet Celesia, Celia (a mutual friend of Scott and Mary Steele), Lady Rowlet, Elizabeth Cooper, Sarah Field, Frances Greville, Lady Catherine Grey, Elizabeth Griffith, Charlotte Lennox, Catharine Macaulay, Elizabeth Montagu, Hannah More, Lady Pennington, Hester Chapone, Catherine Talbot, Anne Steele, Elizabeth Tollett, Phillis Wheatley, Anna Williams, Mary Whateley, and three others. Excluding the unknown trio and Celia, this litany of prominent female intellectuals and writers distinguishes Scott's poem from three of the male authors.' So do her commentaries and approbation of female friendship.[38] Among Scott's special contributions—aside from those on Wheatley, Macaulay, Barbauld, Montagu, Talbot, and Steele already cited—was that on the prominent Charlotte Lennox, who had published many novels and translations in the 1750s and 1760s and had edited *The Lady's Museum* (1760–1761). "One of the most intelligent and valuable early women's magazines,"[39] a contemporary critic called her effort, while James Boswell quoted Samuel Johnson's assertion that "Mrs. Lennox" was "superior" to Fanny Burney, Elizabeth Carter, and Hannah More.

Published in 1755 and again in 1760, Elizabeth Tollett's posthumous poems contained many translations and a long, solid panegyric to women in "Hypatia." This poem about Hypatia, the female philosopher of the title who succeeded "to Plato's chair" induces Tollett to enquire about learning for women:

Or yet is this a Crime? the Mind to raise,
To follow Nature in her winding ways:
To interdicted Knowledge to aspire.[40]

In *Letters on the Improvement of the Mind*, Hester Mulso Chapone champions learning for females while advising young women to use their feelings "to spur [themselves] on to right actions." *Letters* was published the same year as Hannah More's text, *The Search After Happiness*, which promoted "a regard for religion and virtue in the minds of young persons, and . . . an innocent, and perhaps not altogether unuseful amusement in the exercise of recitation."[41] *The Female Advocate* was published the following year. A new cultural agenda focused on females.

Another less obvious text hovers at the edges of Scott's poem. In contrast to her tough-minded demands for women, Scott appeals for sympathy, introducing a gendered, personal note that is singularly absent from male eulogies. Paradoxically (perhaps), this plea for future female learning complements Scott's self-representation as an ailing woman. By inflecting invalidism and blending it with praise for learning, Scott marks the multiple nature of women's lives, their doubled lack of education and medical attention, especially in terms of a "woman's disease." Scott's comments about her condition are unabashed: "Sunk with languor, and unceasing pains,/ Life's purple current stagnates in my veins . . ." The verb *stagnates* and other references to Scott's illness, both in Seward's correspondence and in *The Female Advocate*, raise the question of Scott as a possible victim of undue bloodletting. Considered at the time a panacea and very commonly prescribed, bloodletting fostered further debilitation, a fact unknown, to practitioners and patients alike. If Scott's blood "stagnates," perhaps unsuccessful bleeding purges might have been attributed to "obdurate" blood.[42] In this exposé of vulnerability, Mary Scott connects herself to individuals involved in domestic affairs—primarily women. She cherishes candor, although her private indignation about being so ill, she hints, induced her to write this defense of her foremothers. Thus Scott reconstructs a female cultural lineage to allow for a voice about the politics of sickness.

Beyond that, in mentioning personal problems, Scott's poem takes on the status of a confession while Scott simultaneously confirms herself as a martyr of sorts. Indicting medical practice, she clarifies that she has long been ill with no cure in sight.[43] Yet she downplays that invalid role, only expressing a longing for "sweet retirement's shady bow'rs."[44] Her delicacy, however, only further underscores her self-representation as a physically frail speaker.

Mary Scott's refusal to capitulate to debilitating illness and her insistence on voicing her ailments match her refusal to allow women to be erased from culture. To coin a later phrase, the personal is

political. She signs the importance of female friendship, philanthropy, and the Bluestocking influence while her tributes to Phillis
Wheatley and Catharine Macaulay evince an abolitionist impulse
and a love of patriotism and freedom.

Moreover, in the preface itself, where Scott lambastes patriarchal strictures against female culture, she adds another oppositional
testimony to recent male tributes. Specifically, Scott mentions the
notorious Laetitia Pilkington in the notes, one of the writers whom
John Duncombe singles out for chastisement. In spotlighting Pilkington, who raised contemporary eyebrows with her memoirs, Scott
reminds readers of Duncombe's collective censure of several distinguished women writers: Aphra Behn, Susanna Centlivre, Delarivière Manley, Theresa Phillips, and Lady Vane. Scott's assertive
response is to include all of Duncombe's cultural pariahs.[45]

Scott's conflict between bold plaudits and uncertainty about
her cultural ground surfaces in the mixed response to *The Female
Advocate*. On the one hand, the *Analytical Review* expresses delight
at the vigor of her lines.[46] Similarly, the *Critical Review* praises
Scott's generosity of spirit and innovative commentary:

> We cannot avoid remarking, as a circumstance greatly to the
> honour of Miss Scott, that she celebrates the praises of the most
> eminent even of her contemporary female writers with a degree
> of warmth and generosity that is seldom discovered among
> rival candidates for same. We may add, that, though her pane-
> gyric includes so many respectable names, she never offends us
> with a repetition of the same compliment, but her address is
> equally various, elegant, and poetical.[47]

Just as effusively, *The Gentleman's Magazine* compliments Scott.[48]
The *Monthly Review*, however, demurs at Scott's doubled contention:
women might be gaining a deserved liberty and female education
should be mandatory. The journal further queries the inclusion of
Phillis Wheatley, thus betraying standard prejudices about African
intellectuality: "Surely Miss Scott has impeached her own judgment
in thus associating the celebrated Miss More with the poor negro
girl," whose talent for poetical imitation we mentioned some time
ago!"[49]

Nonetheless, Scott's patriotic paean attracted some followers,
indirectly if not directly. With the publication of *The Female Geniad*
in 1791, thirteen-year-old Elizabeth Benger followed in Scott's footsteps and raised *The Female Advocate* to new radical heights.[50] To
Scott's celebration of Catharine Macaulay, Benger added the names

of Mary Wollstonecraft, Helen Maria Williams, Charlotte Smith, and Elizabeth Inchbald. By then, Mary Wollstonecraft was preparing A *Vindication of the Rights of Woman* for the press and the face of feminist protest would change for good.

The Female Advocate, then, marks an important landmark in eighteenth-century gendered nationalist culture, three-quarters of the way through the century, on the cusp of the French Revolution. Just as importantly, the poem cuts through race and class barriers.

A decade following its publication, Scott wrote one last poem that focused on Jesus Christ but innovatively reevaluated the messiah along national-secular lines. *Messiah, A Poem* (1788)[51] states Mary Scott, was occasioned, "by reading Mr. Hayley's animated exhortation to Mr. Mason to write a National Epic Poem." Scott responded by eulogizing Jesus Christ. In defiance of Unitarian tenets, the unorthodox Scott refers to Jesus' "birth divine" (p. 12). Avarice, "accurst debaser of the mind," never tempted Jesus, who sought only "the woes of men to heal" (p. 29). Foregrounding Christ as a moral paragon rather than God's eternal equal, emphasizing his miracles and Resurrection, Scott abandons contemporary Unitarian tenets.

On a more personal note, Scott's filial obedience played a large role in her life—Scott compliments Jesus for feeling "all filial love's soul—soft'ning power," but cautions him to "let thy heart revere [his Mother] / and thou, my parent, hold him ever dear" (p. 45).

More explicitly than *The Female Advocate*, *The Messiah* opposes imperial predation. First of all, Jesus' first important appearance confirms him as a "messenger of love," someone who wants "remotest nations in one faith to bind" (p. 23). Religious orientation aside, Scott promotes global peace. Moreover, Jesus attacks the Roman invasions as Scott intertextually complicates Britain's contemporary global role. Unlike other individuals who relish complicity and personal advantage, Jesus could not be tempted: "Their soul, by no celestial passions fir'd, / Nought but sublunar wealth and pomp desir'd; / to lay the soaring Roman eagle low, / And to their yoke their proud oppressions bow" (p. 24).

Jesus' statements about Roman imperialism are unequivocal: "Tyrannic man shall then no more controul / God's undivided empire over the soul" (p. 31). Although they welcome his sentiments, when his followers realize that Jesus is a "poor mechanic" or carpenter, their "canker'd minds" are soon furious that such a lowly person claims the status of Messiah (p. 23). Later, when news of the Resurrection spreads, conversion becomes easier and "Rome's polish'd sons their idol gods resign'd / and homage to the living God confin'd"

(p. 51). Thus Jesus' narrative underwrites Scott's apparent antagonism to Roman Catholicism: "Gaunt superstition [with] his giant head (and hypocrisy)" (p.52). Silently challenging imperial predation and greed in the name of Roman Catholic religious beliefs, she condemns the "practice of selling indulgences . . . publicly hawked about the streets by pedlars" (pp. 52–53).

Scott's last lines cry for an end to war, bigotry, and empire:

Hasten, great God! the long-predicted time
When Jesus shall be known in every clime,
When the red torch of war no more shall burn,
Nor feeling hearts o'er slaugher'd millions mourn;
And When, malignant scourge of every age,
Shall bigot fury cease its deathful rage; . . .
When to the child of virtue shall be given,
To find e'en earth the blissful porch of heav'n! (Pp. 54–55)

Closely identified with Mary Scott, the speaker in Part 2 explicitly implores truth (or Jesus / God) to "chase the thick mist of prejudice away . . . let thy heart," the speaker counsels the messiah, "expand with social love" (pp. 31–32). Love of humanity should not be confined only to Britain, "but in its warm embrace enfold mankind" (p.32).

By the end of her life, Mary Scott scarcely conceals the sadness that inflects the *Messiah*. Illness has overtaken her.

In *Messiah*, then, she proffers another offbeat amalgam of personal and political concerns that inscribes her illness. Focusing on an unconventional Jesus enables her to identify with a model figure who, like herself, dies young. His acceptance of an untimely death resonates in her own uneasy acceptance of mortality as her health declines rapidly. Jesus' "strugglings of his soul" find echoes in Scott's own fraught religious conversion in early life.

Beyond inscribing the personal in *Messiah*, Scott attacks prejudice and Roman plunder. As a somewhat feminized Jesus takes time to interact with the daughters of Jerusalem, he deplores the imminent "ravage [of] your devoted land" (p. 43). Social love is the answer.

The Female Advocate stamps Mary Scott as a cultural historian who helps to redefine nation along gendered lines from a progressive Protestant perspective. *The Messiah* reconfigures this gendered commitment into a frontal attack on Roman imperial predation and religious superstition.

Personal circumstances dictate *Messiah* as Scott lies moribund. In this debilitated state, she pens a poem on the eve of her death, "Stanzas Written at Yeovil, 1790."[52] Nothing, she confesses, can any longer bring joy: "Scenes of my Youth that once could please, / Where is your soft Enchantment flown?" She goes on to deplore several deaths: "The social Circle smiles in vain / If absent those the Soul holds dear, / Nor Wit nor Gravity can gain / The Mourner's inattentive ear." Striving for an elusive harmony, Mary Scott's verse reaches personal closure.

CHAPTER FOUR

Ann Yearsley, the Published Writings: Gender, Patriotism, and Resistance

As advocates of a strong national identity, Mary Collier and Mary Scott contributed to cross-class gendered cultural history; they helped to redefine Englishness along these lines. Ann Yearsley, however, took up the case of nation, gender, and class a little differently. Impecunious and soon at odds with her patron, she had to prove herself in a tough market. Unlike Collier, cross-class collaboration ultimately worked against her, or so it seemed. Pronounced a "savage" by her patron, the well-known evangelical writer, Hannah More, Yearsley published a second volume of poems after their irreversible altercation, projecting an undaunted self-image.

Furthermore, she had to justify her status as a milkwoman who published poems, not like Collier, by permitting M. B.'s "authenticating" statements, but by regaling the public with tales of her quarrel with More. In other words, revealing these private matters was an understood mandate for public acceptance and respectability. Refusing to be erased, using her texts as a site of gendered class power, she pressed on as a writer, publishing three volumes of poetry, significant occasional poems, a play, and a novel in just over a decade.

Gradually bracketing arenas of violence and self-love as male, she went on to challenge military aggression, identify with tyrannized people, and advocate rebellion. Yet her relationship to English national identity was complex. Initially she supported the French Revolution, then retreated from that position to support the guillotined monarchs and praise Britain's naval victories. Her conflicts notwithstanding, she prised open a space for a representative cross-class, cross-race female voice. Let me now back up and contextualize Ann Yearsley's intricate personal and public interactions.

45

The connection between Ann Yearsley's personal circumstances and her first volume of poems explains why she veers from the explictly female-based orientation of Mary Collier and Mary Scott. A milkwoman turned poet, Yearsley endured social stigma and contestation all her creative life, best characterized in a published review of her play *Earl Goodwin* (1791). "Nil admirari," the reviewer wrote, "should be the maxim with Reviewers: but when milkwomen write tragedies, is it possible to refrain from a little vulgar wonderment."[1]

Yearsley's unique career began in shocking conditions on the outskirts of Bristol in the harsh winter of 1783–1784.[2] Her entire family—her husband John, four children, and her mother—resigned themselves to almost certain death from starvation at home:[3] "The landlord had taken the cows; the famished husband sat by the hearth of his stripped cottage; old Mrs. Cromartie lay bedridden in a corner on a heap of straw, and the children were crying for food." At that inauspicious time, while Yearsley was pregnant and just over twenty, her husband was, in Hannah More's words, "an honest and sober man," probably an out-of-work agricultural laborer. Her mother lived long enough to see the family rescued by the fortuitous intervention of a local man, Mr. Vaughan, but she died of want almost immediately after.[4]

Months later, Hannah More heard of the family's plight and of Yearsley's poetry. After reading some poems, More offered to be Yearsley's patron, a gesture that assumed the milkwoman's unconditional gratitude and reflected a fashionable eighteenth-century welcome for "untutored genius." More then solicited the help of Elizabeth Montagu, known as "Queen" of the Bluestockings, to facilitate the publication of Yearsley's poems. In a letter to Montagu from Bristol on August 17, 1784, More explained Yearsley's history and circumstances and why she had "adopted" her as a protégée:

I have enquired into her life and Conversation, which I find to be very blameless. She is about seven and twenty, and what will excite your compassion for a Woman of *Sentiment*, was sacrificed for *money* at seventeen to a silly man whom she did not like; the Husband had an Estate of *Six pounds* a year, and the marriage was thought too advantageous to be refused. But misfortunes, six Children, and the Poet's vice, want of Oeconomy, have dissipated this *ample* Patrimony; so that in the severity of last Winter, herself, husband, babes, and her Mother all got together into a Stable—to die of hunger!—the Mother actually perished; the rest were saved by a gentleman accidentally looking into the stable; . . . She assured me . . . that tho' she never allowed herself to look into a book till her work was done and her children asleep, yet in those moments she found that reading and writing cou'd allay hunger and subdue calamity.[5]

In another letter to Montagu a month later, More's condescension toward Yearsley, which was to affect later events, became more pronounced: "I am *utterly* against taking her out of her station. *Stephen* [Duck] was an excellent Bard as a *Thrasher*, but as the Court Poet, and rival of Pope, detestable."[6] On October 22 of the same year, More was once again lauding Yearsley:

> All I see of her, raises my opinion of her genius . . . . I send you a passage or two from a longer Poem, which you will allow to be extraordinary for a milker of Cows, and a feeder of Hogs, who has never *seen* a Dictionary.[7]

In one of her last encomiastic letters on Yearsley's behalf (December 7, 1784), More urged Montagu to obtain as many subscribers as possible to Yearsley's first volume. The book was duly published in 1785 to instant acclaim. A certain public construction of Yearsley's life ensued. What generated such an unusual situation?

Yearsley's creativity was first kindled by her mother as they strolled through Clifton churchyard on Bristol's outskirts, reading verses on tombstones and musing on the dead.[8] Her mother delivered milk door-to-door to Bristol dignitaries during Queen Anne's reign, and borrowed books "from her betters, who kindly lent them."[9] Thus Yearsley remembers her early education in terms of proud maternal care. More's testimony before she and Yearsley quarreled irreconcilably illumines Yearsley's cultural milieu: Yearsley, noted More, had read *Paradise Lost* and Edward Young's *Night Thoughts*, but

> of Pope, she had only seen the Eloisa; and Dryden, Spenser, Thomson, and Prior, were quite unknown to her, even by name. She had read a few of Shakespeare's Plays, and speaks of a translation of the Georgics, which she has somewhere seen, with the warmest poetic rapture.[10]

Critics have noted the considerable impact of Milton on Yearsley's work.[11] With borrowed books, a sharp eye, and the Bristol world for inspiration, Yearsley infused her poetry with powerful feelings, a quest for justice, and an evolving ideological perspective.

Young's thematics appealed to Yearsley's disposition and intellect: she identified, it seems, with his querulous melancholy after 1740, his meditations on death, mutability, the difficulty of advancement, and the nature of ambition.[12] He suggested different ways to explore her rare private and public doubled status as a worker-poet who suffered family trauma.[13] Young's *Conjectures on Original Composition*, in which he extolled the genius of imaginative, innovative, and untutored people, that she might well have read, would have encouraged Yearsley in her poetic practice: "Let us build our compositions," Young proposes, "with the spirit, and in the taste, of the ancients, but not with their materials: . . . All eminence, and distinction, lies out of the beaten road."[14]

Yearsley's first volume, *Poems on Several Occasions* (1785), contained sixteen poems—some to and about aristocratic people—on conventional topics: death, night, solitude, friendship, nature, and charity. Moreover, she prefaced the poems with an autobiographical narrative that addressed an abiding skepticism with middle-class benevolence.

To begin with, in Yearsley's tribute to Stella (More's classical name), who accused Yearsley of flattery, the author denounced the fulsome ingratiation, customarily tendered by a protégée. A fiery self-perception flaunted her class origins:

For mine's a stubborn and a savage will;
No customs, manners, or soft arts I boast,
On my rough soul your nicest rules are lost;
Yet shall unpolish'd gratitude be mine.[15]

In "On Clifton Hill" she aired that same sense of survival and eschewal of niceties: "Half sunk in snow, / Lactilla [Yearsley's classical name], shivering, tends her favorite cow" (p. 108); she also confirmed her solidarity with other laboring women. This bonding gesture that became a common trope of Yearsley's texts punctuated her final poem in *Rural Lyre* eleven years later:

Ye blooming maids, beware
Nor the lone thicket with a lover dare.
No high romantic rules of honour bind
The timid virgin of the rural kind
No conquest o'er the passions e'er was taught, . . .
    Instead, the fear of shame
Proves a strong bulwark, and . . .
Shielded by this, they flout, reject, deny.
        (*Poems on Several Occasions*, p. 111)

Despite restrictions on female behavior, Yearsley urged women to resist imposed constraint: "Sit not within the threshold of Despair, / Nor plead a weakness fatal to the fair" (p. 116). Another self-dramatization as an inspired poet emerged in a poem to her copatron, Elizabeth Montagu. Feeling thwarted, she pondered how creative ideas can dissipate from lack of encouragement. She acknowledges difficulty in voicing inchoate thoughts that are stirred up by a beautiful, natural environment:

> Oft as I trod my native wilds alone,
> Strong gusts of thought wou'd rise, but rise to die. . . .
> My ravish'd soul to extacy untaught, . . .
> All expir'd, for want of powers to speak. (Pp. 104–5)

In 1785, Yearsley's sense of national pride is strong but not yet connected to personal and patriarchal resistance to injustice.

In her poem "To Her Grace the Duchess Dowager of Portland" Yearsley proclaims her public position as an allegedly untutored poet: "O, swell the untaught rapture; bid it rise Spontaneous in my bare uncultur'd mind!" (pp. 97–98). Anything done in the Duchess of Portland's name, from adventures on the Nile or fighting serpents "in Arabian wilds," is worth it. In orientalizing praise of the duchess whose favor facilitates Yearsley's success (as we learn from a footnote in her second volume), Yearsley supports British predations abroad. Her praise of Walpole's novel, *The Castle of Otranto*, matches the aristocratic paean in its sentiment (pp. 87–96). She admires Walpole's wand, his creative endeavor that can cast a spell on readers—its masculinist pun unconscious and unnoted. Walpole's distinct contribution to England's culture inflects the text.

The public enthusiastically responded to her first volume; three editions were printed before she and More parted ways. Although Yearsley could scarcely have predicted either the cause of their disagreement or the risk of co-optation, her poetic self-portrayal as the talented milkwoman who excoriated time-honored knee scraping might well have marked potential trouble to those familiar with More's strictness about class. So, seven months after the publication of the first volume, Hannah More severely criticized Yearsley, for balking at stipulations attached by More to her patronage. More's indignant outburst to Elizabeth Montagu verifies Ann Yearsley's contentions about More's arrogance:

> our unhappy Milkwoman has treated me with the blackest ingratitude. . . . She accused me in the openest and fullest man-

ner of a design to defraud her of the money, and demanded it.
She had before cheerfully signed the deed which impower'd
you, Madam, and me to be Trustees for her Children, lest her
Husband shou'd spend it. . . . Nothing wou'd appease her fury
but having the money to spend, and which she expected in a fit
of vulgar resentment, I shou'd give her, but my sense of duty
will not allow it. Her other charges against me are that I have
spoilt her verses by my corrections, and that she will write
another book directly to show I was of no use to her, that I have
ruined her reputation by the Preface which is full of falsehoods,
that it was the height of insult and barbarity to tell that she
was poor and a Milkwoman. —My dear Madam, I cou'd weep
over our fallen human Nature. . . . I hear she wears very fine
Gauze Bonnets, long lappets, gold Pins etc. Is such a Woman to
be trusted with her poor Children's money?[16]

Yearsley's demands for autonomy struck More (it seems) as
politically dangerous, as well as unbecoming to a milkwoman.[17] But
More's final note that was conveyed by her bookseller, Thomas
Cadell, to a friend of Yearsley and dated from Hampton, January 12,
1786, left Yearsley undaunted. She decided "to publish this fourth
edition [of the first volume after it went out of print] with a faithful
statement of facts as they successively arose." Cadell obliquely
acknowledged the power wielded by More and her evangelical allies
when he informed Yearsley that he "will not engage further with
me." Yearsley's textual footnote supplies a spicy detail to the uproar;
she continued to pick up scraps for her pigs from More's household
cook, a gesture that infuriated More. In their farewell exchange,
More's ethnocentric language and her treatment revalidates Yearsley's charge of More's highhandedness:

The last and final interview between Miss More and me, took
place in July, when three gentlemen were present, . . . Miss
More appeared to be greatly moved, and told me imperiously,
that I was "a savage"—that "my veracity agreed with my other
virtues"—that I "had a reprobate mind, and was a bad woman."

Yearsley's response signs her refusal to be cowed:

I replied, "that her accusations could never make me a bad
woman—that she descended in calling me a savage, nor would
she have had the temerity to do it, had I not given myself that
name!"[18]

Yearsley's public account of the quarrel was treated with so much skepticism—further evidence of class attitudes—that she felt obliged to add a legal deed of trust to her manuscript. This document corroborated Yearsley's published preface and informal statements to friends. In later texts, Yearsley employed the same tactic to protect herself from people similarly attempting to control her. This textual braiding of legal documents and references stemmed from Yearsley's apparent realization, following both her mother's death and her confrontation with Hannah More, that individual solutions to problems did not work; external aid mattered and had to be invoked, wherever possible. More withdrew support of any kind after Yearsley's manifesto. In her texts and in public, milkwoman Yearsley realigned herself with the dispossessed, conscious of her vulnerable economic status as a laboring artist.[19] It turned out that her apprehensions were justified; the majority of More's biographers would portray Yearsley as a willful ingrate.[20]

When Yearsley ventured on a second volume "with as much expedition as the more important duties of my family will permit," help emerged in unexpected quarters.[21] Contemporary Eliza Dawson tells of reading

> somewhere . . . the poor woman's narrative . . . requesting to have the uncontrolled disposal of the interest only of the money which . . . had been raised by subscription for her poems. . . . I thought it showed a case of direct attempt by the strong to oppose the weak . . . and, authorized by my father I wrote to Mrs. Yearsley offering to collect subscriptions for her new volume of poems advertised for publication. . . . Five hundred subscribers I obtained for her. She afterwards addressed some complimentary verses to me in that volume.[22]

At least 450 people subscribed to the volume, including several titled people and dignitaries; the highly respected firm of G. G. & J. Robinson published it and all Yearsley's subsequent volumes until her death. In his reminiscences, Joseph Cottle mentions the fact that a £200 advance from the Robinsons (reputed to be warm-hearted) helped Yearsley to open a circulating library.[23] The affluent bishop of Derry helped with his patronage. These combined efforts enabled Yearsley to recuperate temporarily from More's treatment, but in the long run, class and reputation told against her.

Yearsley's vibrant second volume publicly proclaimed that More had no hand in writing the poems, an aspersion frequently cast against Yearsley. In response, Yearsley inscribed a poetic declaration of independence that encouraged other (potential) male and female worker-poets. The blunt, defiant tone of "To Those Who Accuse the Author of Ingratitude" matched Yearsley's perspective. Her opponents were myopic and disruptive, she asserted, for they viewed the world "thro' optics dim . . . and rend apart from the well-order'd whole." She wryly featured their sensibilities as "low, groveling, and confin'd." Since they discerned only surfaces and never an event's "minutest cause," they could not fathom why "dark afflictions" were visited on the wretch, "inured and patient in the pangs of woe." Likewise, their "incapacious souls" failed to comprehend Yearsley herself, who diverged from "the purer path . . . [for the] Craft's poor dregs" [i.e., poetry]. Theirs was the world of "noos'd opinion." In disparaging their values, Yearsley claimed her own:

> A wish to share the false, tho' public din,
> In which the popular, not virtuous, live;
> A fear of being singular, which claims
> A fortitude of mind you ne'er could boast;
> A love of base detraction, when the charm
> Sits on a flowing tongue, and willing moves
> Upon its darling topic. (Pp. 59–60)

Under the guise of rebuking her opponents, Yearsley charged More with callousness while declining victimage. She declares a personal epistemological revolution. Hannah More has forced new knowledge upon her, new ways of configuring the world, and it is not a pretty picture.

"Addressed to Revenge: A Fragment" further interweaves the relationship between class hegemony and Yearsley's life and art. Calling quiet attention to More's verbal assassinations, Yearsley scoffed at aspersions of vengeance, of being, in More's word, a "savage." Her thoughts transcended such crude banality:

> I charge *thee* not with Inj'ries, 'tis not *thou*
> Canst ease my lab'ring heart: the wounds *I* feel,
> In base *Revenge*, shall never find their cure.
> My soul sits conscious of a nobler claim . . .
>   Her strong height
> Thou *shalt* not reach.—Then flye, fell *Revenge*;
> Seize more defenceless holds, where *Honour* mourns
> Internal desolation. (Pp. 102–3)

She refused to sojourn in revenge's "Malignant empire"—only those who craved "vile Calumny" were authentic clients. The invisible villain could well be Hannah More, the insensitive individual who employed vengeance to "dim the eye / Of Fair Opinion, while her pois'nous dews / Fall heavy on the frugal crop" (p. 103). Few readers could have doubted Yearsley's target, since More's intransigence had forced the scandal. Yearsley insisted on full disclosure.

The poems on ingratitude and revenge contrast with "On the Remembrance of a Mother," where Yearsley's personal agony discreetly manifests itself. The poems prepare us for her assault against slavery two years later. Overwhelming sadness (dreary winter) chilled her creative powers, as her mother slipped into death:

> Thine eye, thine ear,
> Thy long-try'd memory, sentimental pow'rs,
>   All sunk in calm gradation, while the sigh
>   Stole in soft silence from my youthful heart. (P. 162)

Being next to her mother as she died, "down life's descent," horrified her: Ann Yearsley, her husband, four children, and her mother at near expiration in a hovel was the paradigm that urged her art, her angry gloom, and her actions. A bereaved and impotent Yearsley guided the reader to "the grave that op'd beneath." At one with "pining Age" in a powerful identifying moment, Yearsley felt her youth disappear with her mother's life. The speaker invites the reader to consider whether the same people who upbraided her for ingratitude would feel for "the venerable head . . . hoary weakness . . . dear declining Age." Round the hearth with her sons, she heard her mother's "firm precepts vibrate," recalling how contentedly they lived in spite of "life's keen tempest." Her mother's courage empowered her to plumb inner depths, to "rest on virtues all my own."[24]

In a conventional commendatory lyric to Eliza Fletcher Dawson, the former stranger who had generously collected subscriptions for the second volume, Yearsley evinces a rare depth of feeling that doubles as a tribute to female friendship. Not only does Eliza inhabit "the whisp'ring gale," but the power of Eliza Dawson, who "owns my rustic soul," could redirect the elements and dissipate Yearsley's sorrows. Dawson's kindness deeply touched Yearsley, a fact consistent with Yearsley's earlier sense of gratitude to Hannah More and Elizabeth Montagu. Perhaps these extravagant expressions of thankfulness signaled a certain kind of frailty or insecurity, a quiet way of encoding gender. Her thanks to Dawson might also have involved some overcompensation for More's abandonment. Tough-minded and fussy about a forthright self-presentation, Yearsley was a woman positively affected by loving gestures as she was negatively affected by cruelty. Fellow Bristolian and friend Joseph Cottle also testified to receiving lavish appreciation. Further, she named a child Frederick, after her second patron, Frederick Augustus Harvey, bishop of Derry and earl of Bristol. In "Addressed to Ignorance," a poem in the second volume, she blames her emotional excess on a lack of formal education:

> All slight thee; no Beauty e'er boasts of thy pow'r;
> No Beau on thy Influence depends;
> No Statesman shall own thee; no Poet implore,
> But Lactilla and thou must be friends. . . .
>
> While Crito in pomp, bears his burden of books,
> On the plains of wild Nature I'm free. (P. 94)

Additionally, Yearsley connected her creativity to class deprivation, hinting that the intuitive response to inspiration, something she considered "natural," was an unencumbered, accessible poetic act. In a poem, "To Mr. . . . An Unlettered Poet, On Genius Improved," she declares that the "moment" when a poem springs into being finds a stronger reception in "untaught Minds." Yearsley introduces this concept, which matches a familiar eighteenth-century notion of "natural genius," into several poems in the second volume.

> I eager seiz'd, no formal Rule e'er aw'd;
> No Precedent controuled; no Custom fix'd
> My independent spirit: on the wing
> She still shall guideless soar. . . .
>   Deep in the soul live ever tuneful springs,
> Waiting the touch of Ecstasy, which strikes
> Most pow'rful on defenceless, untaught Minds;
> Then, in soft unison, the trembling strings
> All move in one direction. Then the soul
> Sails on Idea, and would eager dart
> Thro' yon ethereal way; restless awhile,
> Again she sinks to sublunary joy. (Pp. 80–81)

This sense of ecstasy seems closely linked to a similar impulse in Romantic poets, as well as to William Collins's concept of inspiration. For Yearsley, self-emanation less than the external environment, or the interaction of consciousness with the external environment, was inspiration's source. Embodying Plato's idea of the poet as one possessed, she acknowledged the limitations and power of natural genius, which often result in an inexplicable missed "connection": "The pen, / Tho' dipp'd in awful wisdom's deepest Tint, / Can *never* paint the wild extatic mood" (pp. 77–78). Contending that no poem is able to reflect poetic inspiration as such, she comes close to saying that she cannot rely on capturing the "moment," that inspiration is phantasmagoric. Paradoxically, then, she demystifies art while claiming for it an intangible, somewhat intuited point of origin. Inspiration and its effect did not constitute the same kind of harmony for Yearsley that Shelley exhibited in his conceptualization of the skylark or Wordsworth with the daffodils. She conceives of inspiration as separate from the poem itself. Thus the act of "creative possession" becomes a quasi-Platonic ideal, and the act of writing a fundamentally physical, human act. Behind those ideas resides a subtle justification for her wide range of subject matter that often includes political and didactic issues. Her attraction to a version of received ideas, "inspiration," and "genius" makes sense. How else could she explain her personal preferences? How hard would it have been in the face of condescension to talk of her mother's cultural influence, her developing taste, her mimetic impulse? In other words, Yearsley strives to explain the contested issue of working people's capacity for creativity. To do so, she claims a metaphysical, hence unprovable inspiration, a quasi-mystical influence: her answer is clever on the face of it, since she invokes an intangible force before which she is helpless. Hence a laboring woman's creativity is not, as was consistently charged, unnatural.

On the other hand, although Yearsley is clearly affected by the concept of untutored genius, she also scorns those who assume she is ignorant. Her poem "Addressed to Ignorance, Occasioned by a Gentleman's desiring the Author never to assume a Knowledge of the Ancients" mocks rich people. As long as she wears the "dark veil" of ignorance, "I can yet keep my way, Still secure from her Critics, or Wits." She invokes ignorance to share her comic reversal of who is ignorant (p. 93). She claims herself free "on the plains of Wild Nature," yet fancy (or imagination) "shews blind Homer" and a host of "Ancients." Thus as she finally puts it, "this age I defy" (p. 99). In other words, she embraces the role of the "uneducated poet" while remaining vividly aware of the value of informal reading.

In a subsequent poem condemning the slave trade, *A Poem on the Inhumanity of the Slave-Trade*, Yearsley changes gears. She employs the concept of social love—by which she means that individuals act everywhere out of love—to explain the need for abolition. Without social love, she ventures, Hannah More's antagonism makes sense. The concept of global harmony punctuated Yearsley's earlier volumes although she defined social love then as synonymous with friendship and charity, little more. Later broadened to stress human connectedness, the concept of social love then saturates Yearsley's texts.

This concept matches the counsel of Mary Scott's speaker: "let thy heart expand with social love" (*Messiah*, p. 32). Focusing on a captured African slave named Luco, the poem against the slave trade raises Yearsley's attacks on injustice to an international level. Her experiences with extremity enable her to identify with corruption on a world wide basis. Hailing from Bristol, a major slave-trading center, she opens her poem by ridiculing those who deny that slaves could be Christians. Rejecting the idea that the distance from a problem should be in inverse proportion to the human concern expended on it, she chooses "Heav'n-born Liberty" as her yardstick. Nature must follow Liberty (advice she followed herself) or the abuse of power "drags on his bleeding victims."

The narrative voice and vantage point indistinguishable from her own, Yearsley addresses issues of marginality, bondage, and the double-edged strictures of custom and law that white women and African slaves faced in different contexts.

The speaker's exhortatory opening lines contrast Bristol's past, "thine heart hath throbb'd to glory," with Bristol's present: "Slaves,/ E'en Christian slaves, have shook their chains, and gaz'd / With wonder and amazement on thee."[25] Iconographically, "the guileful crocodile's" tears underscored the hypocrisy of Bristol's church-going slave traders. She then apostrophizes "souls who feel for human woe" by elaborating on the ubiquitous knotted whip. Imaging slaves who patiently forgive and the crafty merchant who "grasps / The wish'd for gold, purchase of human blood!" (p. 7), she enjoins readers to take sides: to oppose, sympathize, and act. She narrates a Manichean tale of good versus evil, the former technically Christians while the latter are technically heathens who scarcely speak English. Nonetheless, Yearsley's ventriloquizing accentuates conventional attitudes that stamped white abolitionist writing. Africa is persistently configured as "barb'rous"; colonial planters are sadists who prolong Luco's final torture after he fights back. The speaker queries the meaning of Christianity while slavery exists, the more so since people living on other continents exhibit more humanity:

Where is your true essence of religion? . . .
Your God
Ye rob of worshippers, his altars keep
Unhail'd, while driving from the sacred font
The eager slave, lest *he* should hope in *Jesus*.

Is this your piety? Are these your laws,
Whereby the glory of the Godhead spreads
O'er barb'rous climes? Ye hypocrites, disown
The Christian name, nor shame its cause. (P. 22)

After a chilling middle section describing atrocities—"the savage
tribes / Are angels when compared to brutes like these"—she
applauds Christian values (p. 25). A final peroration acts as a bulwark against greed and murder. Patriotism and a concern for the
afterlife could dissolve unconscionable evil:

Advance, ye Christians, and oppose my strain:
Who dares condemn it? Prove from laws divine,
From deep philosophy, or social love,
That ye derive your privilege. I scorn
The cry of Av'rice, or the trade that drains
A fellow-creature's blood: . . . Curses fall
On the destructive system that shall need
Such base supports! Doth England need them? No;
Her laws, with prudence, hang the meagre thief
That from his neighbour steals a slender sum,
Tho' famine drove him on. O'er *him* the priest,
Beneath the fatal tree, laments the crime,
Approves the law, and bids him calmly die. (Pp. 25–27)

Yearsley ends by apostrophizing social love. Implicitly she
demands abolition while chiding Hannah More for religious hypocrisy and lack of love. Readers—not just plantocrats—must "loose the
fetters" of their minds as they respond:

Hail, social love! true soul of *order*, hail!
Thy softest emanations, pity, grief,
Lively emotion, sudden joy, and pangs,
Too deep for language, are thy own: then rise,
Thou gentle angel! . . .
To banish Inhumanity. Oh, loose
The fetters of his mind, enlarge his views,
Break down for him the bound of avarice, . . .
He shall melt,
Yea, by thy sympathy unseen, shall feel
Another's pang: for the lamenting maid
His heart shall heave a sigh; with the old slave
(Whose head is bent with sorrow) he shall cast

His eye back on the joys of youth, and say,
"Thou *once* couldst feel, as I do, love's pure bliss;
"Parental fondness, and the dear returns
"Of filial tenderness were thine, till torn
"From the dissolving scene." —Oh, social love,
Thou universal good. (Pp. 28–29)

Once social love operates, malice will dissolve. Collective love will "touch the soul of man; / Subdue him; make a fellow-creature's woe / His own by heart-felt sympathy, whilst wealth / Is made subservient to his soft disease" (p. 30). Her last couplet anticipated a Bristol that would fill Yearsley and other Bristolians with pride: "And when thou hast to high perfection wrought / This mighty work, say, *such is Bristol's soul*" (p. 30).

By challenging the complicity of Bristol's inhabitants, Yearsley exposes contradictions between rulers and toilers; she excoriates relationships where power exists unevenly—where slaves are pitted against buyers, planters, overseers, and the allied personnel of British colonialism. Abhorring helpless victimage, she proposes rebellion as a solution. Thus Yearsley subtly asserts female moral superiority and political awareness. Luco himself epitomizes a virtuous female victim who is linked with charity and tolerance. His violent response constitutes a salutary reminder that women could subvert prescribed roles and values when they chose.

Two years later, in *Stanzas of Woe*, Yearsley intensifies her battle against class-biased attitudes by indicting a cold-blooded mayor and lamenting a viciously precipitated miscarriage. "Independence . . . thou Stubborn God! / Alone ador'd by bold Immortal Spirit!" is the speaker's (Yearsley's) theme as she scorns "the gaudy Fool, the pale insidious Slave" who accepts dependence. In the prefatory "Advertisement," she explains that her twelve- and nine-year-old sons were playing during the 1789 hay harvest in the fields of Levi Eames, the late mayor of Bristol. Because the boys trespassed on private property, one of Eames's footmen whipped them viciously. Outraged, the author was advised by her lawyer not to pursue the matter because her class placed her at a disadvantage. Several nights later, the second son, who had previously quarreled with the footman about his brutal actions, was ambushed at Eames's door and beaten until he could not stand. Yearsley reacted by pressing charges against the footman. When she asked him in court if he would have murdered the boy, the footman replied that the point of his punishment was to ensure no repetition. Probably for pecuniary reasons, Yearsley's lawyer advised her to drop the case.

Relaxing at her front door the following year, Ann Yearsley watched a man chasing unknown children from his fields. After they eluded him, he verbally "treated her in a vulgar opprobrious manner," the shock of which caused her to miscarry that night.

With harshly ironic resonances, Yearsley dedicated *Stanzas of Woe* to Eames:

Sir,

Should your Friends stand amazed at your receiving a *Dedication* I beg you will apologize for *me*, and say it is the first offering I have ever laid on the Altar of *Insolence*. Through this little Poem you will find the language of Sorrow and Indignation alternately prevail; I hope you accept it properly, not *exultingly*; though I am well convinced of your reliance on the infallibility of that benevolent rule, viz.

"What we give to the poor, we lend to the Lord,"—Yea, even an Horsewhip!

With due respect / My Children and Self are, / Sir, / Your very humble Servants, / Ann Yearsley, &c.&c.

The poem began, she notes parenthetically, "the first morn [after the miscarriage] of the Physician's allowing the air to play through the Author's window."[26] Craving "balmy air" to dispel the "mental agony [that] devours my heart," she wryly invites Eames to consider his boyhood pleasures while she meditates on grief. Did he (like her sons) "stretch . . . careless on the new-mown hay"? In recompense, was his "skin by cruel lashes torn"?

Yet these are ills that on my children fall,
    And fall from *Thee*, thou *Draco*, of the age!
Their feeble cries shall for my vengeance call,
    And fill my soul with wild, eternal rage. (P. 3)

By comparing Eames to Draco, a seventh-century Athenian lawgiver noted for legal severity, Yearsley equates them.[27] Let him be wary—she warns—of the "maternal agony high in her veins"; his power cannot control her "fierce wrath":

Insolent Tyrant! humble as we are,
    Our minds are rich with honest truth as thine;
Bring on thy sons, their value we'll compare,
    Then—lay thy infant in the grave with mine. (P. 4)

A derisive Yearsley reminds readers that Eames's class position had shielded him from prosecution. Infuriated by Eames's immunity that denied her "all hope of publick right," she pursues him with mocking questions. She reminds readers that "From true Religion tortures never flow," an argument she articulated in her antislavery poem against pseudo-Christian merchants and slave traders. Since the Magna Carta had not sanctioned such violations, Eames belongs "In Pluto's dark dominion [where] thy laws [shall] be read; and guilty spirits deck thy brow" (p. 7).

Thus the poet ponders inner conflict and "my infant slain." Lashing Eames with her anger, she invites him to "lay thy infant in the grave with mine." How is Eames any different, Yearsley implies, from plantocrats who separate families, flog pregnant women, and rape female slaves. He holds the lives of infants and pregnant women in contempt. At the end, her anger muted, she can dispel sadness by musing on the "eternal *Cause*," by humbly requesting the air to waft her "dying infant" to God.

Yearsley's defiance of Eames provoked a sequel that vindicated her earlier charge: the contemptuous treatment she received was due to her class and gender. Yearsley's response resembled her indignant response to More's subvention of her profits while also underwriting Yearsley's willingness to disregard consequence in fighting for principle.

Shortly after, when Yearsley wrote an ode to support a hospital benefit, several of Eames's supporters threatened to withdraw their subscriptions. Yearsley responded boldly to this attempted censorship by publicly exposing them. In *The Dispute: Letter to the Public from the Milkwoman*,[28] she baited Sir Stivvy Nicholson, Eames's "sneering Attorney," dissociating herself from the taint of unjust authority: "I wish to devote a few moments to my valuable Friends, not to make a concession to my Enemies; to the former class *every thing* is due—to the latter *nothing* (p. 3). She configures Eames as an accomplice in the horsewhipping and the suppression of her ode. Disdaining their importunities, she expresses shock and disbelief that "Any Body of *Gentlemen* would act so *unmanly* as to form a *terrific party* against a poor *Milkwoman*. . . . Have I wrested the Horsewhip from his hand? . . . Why should your *Gentlemen* Subscribers point their Artillery against One who has *laboured in the Vineyard* as well as Mr. Eames?" (pp. 6–7). When her lawyer, a Mr. Kift, demurs at disclosing the names of the "Gentlemen," she explodes: "Will you stand the Champion of distressed Males?" She advises him instead to "comfort the *Ladies*, it is but fair to let *me* take care of the *Gentlemen*" (p. 7). An italicized postscript reads: "*I expect an Answer,*

Sir." The names that Kift later sent turned out to include those of a churchman, a tradesman, and a "Knight of *the Order of the Petticoat*." Cynically musing aloud about who would defend her against church and state opposition, Yearsley published their full names in *The Dispute*, noting that "the tremendous Fiat of ten Men, shall *give*, and *take away*." Jeering at their "superior Influence and Power . . . [their] *Sentiment* and *Taste*," she highlights the so-called individual freedom enjoyed in the city of Bristol. Yearsley's diatribe against Hannah More and her sallies against the slave trade indict that town: she calls for a home town "cleansing." In a sense, she becomes Bristol's moral representative. Mocking a lawyer who claimed she would be sued for libel, she shrewdly advises him to check the third statute of the Mercian Code of Laws, which states "that to call a Man by his proper Name is no libel" (p. 8).

In four crowded years of energetic confrontation, Yearsley had questioned diverse forms of authority. She defended herself against Hannah More as a disadvantaged female worker; in *Stanzas* and *The Dispute* she maintained this stance, squaring off against the mayor and powerful local church and state dignitaries. In the antislavery poem, she contested the question of rights and Britain's global predations. Once again she allied herself with victims.

In *Earl Goodwin*, a play performed in 1789 and published in 1791, Yearsley pursues allied concerns, turning her attention more noticeably to royal and national authority, to the cause of women and peasants just prior to the Norman Conquest in 1066.[29] Moreover, although Yearsley shifts the site of the struggle, she continues to expose gender and class inequity. During these years, patriotic sentiment and a sense of national identity were common. By 1789, in Gerald Newman's words, "the making of English nationalism was over." Newman goes on to define a radical "Saxon" ideology of freeborn English people around 1789. Their characteristics would be populist, monarchical, anti-aristocratic, antiforeign, antirepublican, "wedded to the myth of the Norman yoke and of an egalitarian social compact in the halcyon pre-Norman days of King Alfred, framed on a dualistic social theory pitting 'People' against tyrannical usurpers."[30]

The play cobbles sections from earlier narratives into one whole narrative piece, a literary patchwork quilt on the *topos* of tyranny.[31] At some levels, the subjugated status of two female protagonists echoes Yearsley's. The silent, applauded peasants are incarnations of Yearsley's sons and African slaves—the same victims but different individuals, maimed and exploited in diverse ways on different continents, in eras six centuries apart.

Written the year after the ode, Yearsley's play excoriates the Roman Catholic Church and state rulers, and champions freedom fighter Earl Goodwin, who sought the restoration of an English monarchy and justice for the dispossessed. In the year that witnessed the outburst of the French Revolution, Yearsley explicitly espouses nationalism. She also applauds the confrontation of "free-thinking" French insurgents against a Roman Catholic bureaucracy. The preface "to the Impartial Reader" discloses her political and anti-Roman Catholic intent: "In more early ages the chain of Superstition fell heavy on the People of England; learning was confined within the cloister, among the frozen, yet ambitious Monks; and the man who dared trust his reason or his faith beyond priestly rule, was pronounced an alien to God and Society." Englishness is specifically opposed to Roman Catholic "foreignness," in 1790 an early allusion to France; benevolence faces off against tyranny.

In the prologue, Yearsley compares her wandering, inspired self to Shakespeare:

With *fancy'd joy* and *real woe* her own . . .
Sudden the light'ning of bright fancy came . . .
But ah! in silence must those raptures die?
Unfed by art?

Like Yearsley, Shakespeare was a "natural" poet who voiced the nation, its warriors, and its needs. He spoke for Englishness versus Frenchness. Yearsley's firm answer proclaims confidence in her home town:

Perish the thought! Here manly sense shall stand, . . .
Here *public candour*, lifting *genius* high,
Shall prove that *Bristol* is her friendly sky.

"Active virtue" alone, insists the speaker, "can be right," and she pleads with Bristol to act positively: "Protect the Muse, who flies the gloomy grove, / To seek the bosom warm'd by Social love." If the muse failed her, there was always "her milking pail." Despite a self-effacing stance, Yearsley has brought gender inequities and caprice into the open; legal restrictions on sexuality and arranged marriages similarly offend her.

In the play's preface, Yearsley quietly alludes to her moral victory against Hannah More while identifing herself with the earl "for his contempt of absurd austerities and *unholy slavery* . . . such feeble efforts [to brand, accuse, and attack Goodwin] shall never arrest the generous current of my thought, when I would defend *an injured*

Reputation." In an "Exordium" that follows after the two-page prologue, she explains that trial by fire was legal during the reign of Edward I (1042–1066), also known as Edward the Confessor. The monarch allied himself with the Normans, whom he had invited back from Normandy after his exile and installed in powerful church and state positions. In terms of Englishness itself, another well-known sobriquet of Edward I was "The Hammer of the Scots" because his armies ravaged Scotland during his reign. Abhorring usurpation at the personal and political levels, Yearsley could find only the Queen Mother, Queen Emma, demonstrating any "miraculous proof of virtue." Conventionally good men—corrupt Normans in this case—tortured innocent women. Yearsley's concluding apology to the "ladies" in the audience for staging "a play without *Love*" acknowledges and perhaps disparages female cultural expectations; it also parades her reluctance to comply. In Yearsley's canon, Queen Emma is another victim turned rebel.

The play opens with Earl Goodwin's warning that no woman—whether "dow'rless maids, unjoyful widows, or the faithful wife"—is safe in Edward the Confessor's England. The earl's son, Harold, blames Queen Emma's trial on the fact that the peers are Norman, not Saxon; ethnicity is the issue. The Saxons marvel at Queen Emma's sturdy refusal not to appeal the trumped-up charge of adultery with the bishop of Winchester. After the monks condemn her to ordeal by fire, the king upholds their judgment against his mother. Harold urges Earl Goodwin to wage war, but Goodwin fears for his daughter, Editha, who is Edward's wife and queen. Harold argues that the wrongs suffered by Editha offer additional reason why war should be urged against Edward. Another son, Tostie, exhorts the earl not to "perish mid the herd / Of sickly slaves who shake the chain and smile" (p. 27). Admonishing his son not to mix personal grievance with national necessity, Earl Goodwin counsels patience. For the time being, he distinguishes injustice against Queen Editha and themselves from crimes committed against a "guiltless nation."

Shortly afterward, Edward I accuses Queen Editha of loving someone else, whereupon the queen denounces arranged marriages, in contrast to marital choices that still remain available to rural women. This reference might recall Yearsley's own circumstances, since her family seems to have arranged her marriage as a young woman to John Yearsley.[32]

Multiple subjugations and responses to them intersect throughout the third act. By the end, the opposition leader, the archbishop of Canterbury, is exiled, both women are openly vindicated, peasants sue for her cause while the struggle over filial duty continues. Yearsley's message is plain. Any individual—whether peasant, baron, or queen—must resist domination at the hands of Roman Catholic foreigners. By analogy, Yearsley lauds the French revolutionary victory while approbating British nationalism and one of its warriors. Earl Goodwin and French revolutionaries are indistinguishable for the time being.

Political messages surge thick and fast as the play speeds to a Hamlet-like conclusion. The Queen Mother reminds King Edward that ends cannot justify means: "who hopes to gain a distant scene of bliss, / Forgetful of the means . . ." (p. 59). She rejects his charge that she lacks spiritual value by castigating the moral bankruptcy of displaying the "form without the essence." After an armed insurrection, Canterbury is dead, Alwine is an ecclesiastical hero, while the contesting earl celebrates, having "Pluck'd off the galling chain of proud oppression / And bade the bending wretch look up to freedom" (p. 69).

In a postlude following the earl's death by poison, an ashamed King Edward withdraws, and Alwine spares the villain's life in deference to the martyred earl's dying wish. Yearsley's dilemma marks a certain naïveté: "I know not whether I am right or wrong in saving the life of [villainous] Lodowicke. I own that such are my feelings towards my fellow creatures, that I think *remorse* worse than *death*: it is to the criminal a torture all his own, while it leaves no blemish on society." Backing up Yearsley's statement is the epilogue, written by a Mr. Meyler; it attacks religion and male tyranny, praises just rebellion, motherhood, and the French Revolution. The Lord Chamberlain censored the six italicized lines as opposition to the French Revolution hardened among conservatives:

> Priestcraft, avaunt! avaunt, *Rebellion*, too!
> We've done, thank Heav'n, at present, Sirs, with you; . . .
>   What a weak head this pious Edward had!
> A monarch, made by priests and friars mad.
> What! let an aged mother shoeless trot,
> To try her virtues over ploughshares hot! . . .
>   But, thank my stars, that Superstition's train
> O'er all the globe is in a rapid wane.
> *Lo! the poor Frenchman, long our nation's jest,*
> *Feels a new passion throbbing in his breast;*
> *From slavish, tyrant, priestly fetters free,*
> *For VIVE LE ROI, cries VIE LA LIBERTE!*
> *And, daring now to ACT, as well as FEEL,*
> *Crushes the convent and the dread Bastile!*

Yearsley's battle cry for liberty and the permission she presumably grants for the inflammatory epilogue to be attached to her play come together at a crucial political moment. Fearless about public censure, she extols the French Revolution at a slant.

Yearsley's temporary pro-French sentiment allies her with radicals and scuttles her career. Anything gallophilic was eventually pronounced criminal; English radicals were roundly condemned by the end of the 1790s. Yearsley's oblique francophilia contrasts sharply with More's gallophobia in *Strictures* (1790), when she condemns "principles and practices of *modern* France."[33] Yearsley, on the other hand, seems to support the French peasantry in their fight against overlords, a class identification that comes easily. She also lambastes Roman Catholicism in her endorsement of Meyler's sardonic usage of "the convent" and "Superstition's train." In concert with these views, the brave Earl Goodwin leads the peasants to revolt against a corrupt monarchy.

Following the publication of *Earl Goodwin* in 1791, Ann Yearsley sought new ways to earn a living that matched her status as a relatively well-known poet. By 1793 she had opened a circulating library in the well-heeled end of Bristol, the fashionable Bristol Hot Wells. Flourishing for several years, it provided a financial haven for Yearsley during the lean years of the revolution and Napoleonic wars.[34] Meanwhile, the *Monthly Review* and *Critical Review* published serious considerations of her texts.

That same year, Yearsley's political views shifted from radical to more conservative, a move that located her alongside the majority of the population. By then, Britain had declared war on France and formed the First Coalition. Prime Minister William Pitt had suspended habeas corpus and had hurriedly secured legislation to prohibit public meetings for fear of working-class insurrection; the London Corresponding Society and other radical groups were now proscribed. Thomas Paine was already in France, fleeing prosecution for the *Rights of Man*.

With the declaration of war, the mood of the country changed. Yearsley joins in the protests at the deaths of the king and queen. Perhaps her precarious class position induced her to play it safe. Possibly her brother and son were soldiers. Napoleon's adoption of a moving column of soldiers rather than a rigid line formation also dealt a blow to British national pride. As Napoleon won one military victory after another, domestic opposition to France solidified. Yearsley's published poems on King Louis XVI and Marie Antoinette mark her evolving patriotism.[35] She blames the king's death on

fancied Liberty, with rude Excess
[that] courts Man from sober Joy, and lures him on
To frantic War, struck by her gaudy Dress,
His ardent Soul is in the Chace undone.
    ("Reflections on the Death of Louis XVI," p. 5)

Is it not ironic, the speaker asks, that freedom fighters perpetuate murder in liberty's name? Yet, liberty is "Like Echo, she exists in airy Sound, / Never possess'd, ne'er to one Rule confin'd" ("Reflections," p. 6).

But Yearsley does equivocate on backing the "ill-fated Louis"; "is it good," inquires the anonymous title page stanza,

For Man to drain the sacred Stream of Life
From his sad Brother's Heart? O tis a Deed
Unworthy an immortal Spirit! where
Shall meek neglected Mercy find a Spot
To weep in Silence o'er her slaughter'd Sons!

Misunderstood liberty might ironically be the culprit:

Yet for this Vapour, gen'rous Man must die,
For this, he ventures on a World unknown;
For this, he braves the Crime of sanguine Dye;
For this, he drags a Monarch from his Throne. (P. 6)

In "Sequel to Reflections on the Death of Louis XVI," the speaker condemns the royal guillotining and especially the fact that the sovereigns' children witness the killing: "*Fury*! thou Curse! . . . / to burn the Brain, and make Thy Vot'ries red, / With Crimson Guilt, at which their Children Start" ("Sequel," p. 4). Despite his death, "martyr'd *LOUIS*" will hear a "sacred Song," inspired by virtue, truth, and order, which "The Sons of Social Love, shall oft relate . . . / Shall touch the Mem'ry with a Monarch's Fate" ("Sequel," p. 7). The speaker's sympathy for the king matches feelings for the queen: "How may I stay pale Murder's ruthless Hand! / How plead with Men, who Mercy most despise!" ("An Elegy on Marie Antoinette of Austria, Ci-Divant Queen of France," p. 3).

The volume that contains the queen's elegy also contains "Poem on the Last Interview between the king of Poland and Loraski."[36] In the course of their interview, Loraski requests permission to commit suicide rather than be enslaved by Russia: "Her Chains are round our lofty turrets thrown" (p. 9). The king denounces the greed of tyrants to Loraski. "Empire, Loraski, is the Tyrant's Boast" (p. 13). Bent on suicide to preserve his honor, the warrior wishes only that his legacy will not die:

> Where dwells, we cry, the great omniscient Mind?
> Could brave LORASKI'S Soul this Being find?
> Yes, as an Atom sails along the Air,
> Attracted tow'rds its own congenial Sphere;
> Or unresisting (by Omniscience hurl'd)
> LORASKI helps to make that THING—A WORLD. (P. 15)

Yearsley spotlights suicide as courage in the face of oppression. The triumphant warrior has earned the right to choose his own death. Deploring the expropriation of Poland, Yearsley signs imperial Russia as the villain who forces Loraski's hand.

Two years later, Yearsley published a historical novel entitled *The Royal Captives*, based on the tale of the man in the iron mask. Since she received £200 for the novel, a decent payment for the time, her reputation had clearly survived. In her last volume of poems, *The Rural Lyre*, which appeared in 1796, she continued to assail tyranny.[37] In that volume, Yearsley ideologically pinpoints changes on the map of Europe during the 1790s. She also addresses a common radical reconstruction at that time of a mythical heritage among ancient Britons.[38]

Put another way, *The Rural Lyre* identifies Ann Yearsley as a proponent of English national identity. Perhaps most noticeably in the poem entitled "To Mira on the Care of her Infant," written in Bristol Wells in September 1795, Yearsley represents her political reorientation. An unconfirmed rumor that one of her sons may have died in battle could explain the condemnation of war. The opening choreographs Yearsley's contestation with war and transnational strife:

> Whilst war, destruction, crimes that fiends delight,
> Burst on the globe, and millions sink in night;
> Whilst here a monarch, there a subject dies,
> Equally dear to him who rules the skies;
> Whilst man to man oppos'd wou'd shake the world,
> And see vast systems into chaos hurl'd,
> Rather than turn his face from yon dread field,
> Or, by forgiving, teach his foe to yield:
> Let us, whose sweet employ the Gods admire,
> Serenely blest, to softer joys retire! (P. 113)

The narrator spells out a certain consolation in the midst of all the turmoil: "We'll nurse the infant, and lament the fire" (p. 114). Deploring male military aggression, Yearsley features a gendered concept of war. Women, she avows, are not "naturally" drawn to such violence:

> We are not made for Mars; we ne'er could bear
> His pond'rous helmet and his burning spear;
> Nor in fierce combat prostrate lay that form
> That breathes affection whilst the heart is warm. . . .
> (Pp. 113–114)

Nonetheless, the speaker patriotically images men at war as "heroes" who have temporarily "retired" from their homes. The baby's father, Amyntor, will be mourned while he fights abroad: "The absent fire ensures / Thy constant memory" (p. 114).

Denouncing military discipline as inimical, the speaker feels unequal to the scale of combat:

> I am no Amazon; nor would I give
> One silver groat by iron laws to live.
> Nay, if, like hers, my heart were iron-bound,
> My warmth would melt the fetters to the ground. (P. 114)

Yearsley reaccentuates her support for the British navy in two major poems, the opening poem "Brutus" and "The Genius of Britain," from which the frontispiece comes. In the author's preface to "Brutus," Yearsley discusses national epics:

> The *Aenead* is not so eventful, nor so interesting, but that an Epic Poem from the History of England might vie with it. If the Author may presume to offer an opinion, her opinion will be, that some of the greatest geniuses of this island neglect the choice of subjects left behind to their learning and their natural powers.

She concocts the mythological story of Brutus, great grandson of Aeneas, landing unexpectedly in Britain with his navy.

This poem is part of an evolving declaration of national identity. The iconic John Bull had emerged as the preeminent representation of that phenomenon in midcentury. Casting Brutus as an ancient patriot-Briton paralleled this popular focus.[39] Brutus, moreover, signified the adoption of a theory about an idyllic Anglo-Saxon

England. In *The History of England from the Revolution,* historian Catharine Macaulay asserted that the "Saxon constitution . . . effectively secured every privilege it bestowed."[40] Known as the *Norman Yoke* theory, it asserted that Anglo-Saxon England was a time of widespread liberty. Saxon institutions spelled freedom until William the Conqueror and his forces invaded.[41] Eventually, Brutus's subscription to pacifism earns him leadership of the Britons, at which point Yearsley foregrounds her concept of social order. An antidote to anarchy and unlike war, which is a "stern foe to social good," social love incorporates ideas of mercy, "boundless Love, Concord, harmonious Liberty and Peace" (p. 16). "Social bands" appear in two manifestations with a "warlike spear" seeking to extirpate anarchy and "humanize the mind" (pp. 6–10). Liberty wants to midwife "social virtues" and foster "Union, my great Palladium" (p. 10). Britons are

Gigantic mortals, painted red and green.
Around the waist huge serpents seem'd to twine,
Sun, moon, and stars on their large bosoms shine:
Wolves, tigers, objects of uncouth delight,
On their wide shoulders dar'd the mimic fight.
The left arm rais'd to point the ruthless dart,
Reveal'd a *lion* couching near the heart (p. 11).

The British swains tremble

who mark the omens of the hour,
Conclude the rip'ning torrent soon must pour;
Tremble lest lightnings with their harvest play,
Or the black daemons swept their all away. (P. 16)

The character in the poem named Liberty puts in a good word for Britons to the skeptical Brutus:

My Britons are not slaves:
There lives no conqueror but the man who saves.
Untaught, unpolish'd is the savage mind,
Yet firm in friendship, to affliction kind. (P. 17)

Eventually Brutus presides over the untamed country and its inhabitants: "He led her forth where rose an infant town, / Long since the seat of science and renown" (p. 25). Then he dies following his victory, "in Order's silken band the Briton's mind" (p. 26), while Liberty begs Jove to tend the warriors (this action appears as the frontispiece of the volume):

"Eternal love," she cried, *"be these thy care!"* . . .
Again her sons arose, and call'd for arms—
Her hair dishevell'd, on her cliffs she stood;
Reclaim'd her empire o'er the briny flood.
Neptune arise, his ev'ry wave uncurl'd:
The Britons seiz'd the trident of the world.
Venus and Jove smil'd from their brightest sphere,
And Godlike order fix'd her standard here.

After the national epic, "Brutus," comes "The Genius of England," a plea to Genius (i.e., the guardian of Britain) to guide the navy safely. This poem intertextualizes popular facts about combat in 1795–1796, when Britain's pride and military advantage lay in its navy. Following Admiral Howe's victory in 1794, Britain maintained naval supremacy, boasting of 158 ships at the start of the war to 80 owned by France. By 1800, the number of British ships rose quickly to 202 while France's declined to 39.[42]

Entitled in full, "The Genius of England, on the Rock of Ages, Recommending Order, Commerce and Union to the Britons," the poem capitalizes on national pride by suggesting that liberty guides the navy and its sailors. Britain's genius urges respect and reiterates that time has removed the people from a state of barbarism and rendered them "civilized," a fraught word in Yearsley's era as now. This national guardian craves the same social order that Yearsley had recommended earlier.

Having triumphantly circulated "blooming commerce" round the world (p. 95), the genius comments:

He grew with you.
His brothers, fairer than the tribes of Ind,
Lav'd desolated shores for you: explor'd,
Busily patient, mines tremendous;—realms
Where Liberty, Religion, and the Name
We love and fear, were strangers. . . .

Praising Britain's global conquests in 1795, Yearsley argues an equally conventional, ethnocentric perspective in "The Genius," similarly evident in the antislavery poem of 1788:

On his tongue,
Unvers'd in flatt'ry, Freedom, born of Law,
Sat ever, to the Pagan yielding much,
Lest charity, philanthropy, and love,

Should blush for his defect—Unfinish'd man,
Produc'd when Nature dallied with employ . . .
A ship-wreck'd stranger as he rov'd
Deep vales of Afric', gathering as he went
Fair truths of intellect, that blaze the mind,
Irradiate mem'ry, and instruct your babes,
When on the floors of Albion. From his form
Gigantic to their view the pigmy maids
Fled trembling; yet with insect skill contriv'd
Nets for his hair, rare sandals for his feet,
Canopy of light rushes, so contriv'd
By secret means . . .
To consolate the awful rover. (Pp. 96–97)

Since the enemies of this loving order lurk everywhere, and
children cannot survive spiritually without it, the country is in a
sorry state:

Envious men
Inquisitive, to draw the guiltless heart
Within their snares, would, like gaunt wolves, deface
The charms of Order. Children, misinform'd,
All you can know of God, you must behold
Through Order: ever-blessed peace and love,
Mercy, benevolence,
That flame so pure,
So little understood, mild charity
And her true attributes. (Pp. 97–98)

This patriotic spirit blesses the navy for alerting the nation:

Women and men, my family of Britons,
Deface not Order! Guard your infant race!
Increasing loves shall pillow them, whilst you
Stand on the rocks of Albion, nor retire
Till your complaining spirits are convinc'd,
The union I commend, is *liberty.* (P. 99)

Poems on contemporary events in *Rural Lyre* chart the long
drawn-out military engagement and Yearsley's ardent commitment
to British policy and British soldiers. As the war drags on, however,
despite her accord with government policy, she adopts a more paci-
fist position; Yearsley's antimilitary assault in "Mira" marks this

evolution. More to the point, as involvement in the war, the "Terror," and unrest persist while more lives—including possibly her brother's—are lost or permanently damaged, Yearsley's opposition strengthens. In these circumstances, the waste of it all becomes a more appropriate discourse. Thus the frontispiece to *Rural Lyre* of the character of Liberty, engraved by Yearsley's son, comes as no surprise—this same Liberty restores Britain to Brutus and guards the nation from French encroachment.

With "An Indifferent Shepherdess to Colin," Yearsley ends on a detached, self-preserving note. A woman tending sheep expresses nonchalant feelings toward a swain named Colin. Ostensibly she rejects Colin's overtures because she knows acceptance will relegate her to a more subordinate status. Colin's proposals should embarrass him, she hints, since seduction would rob her of autonomy: "Go home, my friend, and blush / For love and liberty." Tuning her "rural lyre" on the mountain top, she teaches Colin inner peace. His servile, vain response devastates her as an individual whose "eternal plan / Is to be calm and free. / Estrang'd from tyrant man / I'll keep my liberty" (p. 141).

In inimitable fashion, Yearsley complicates the notion of women's independence by attributing it to an indifferent shepherdess. An earlier poem in *Poems on Various Subjects*, entitled "Indifference" extolled the same concept. A "foe to sharp sensation," an "antidote to pain," indifference substitutes for patience. Providing comfort, it eases

> The Soldier's toil, the gloomy Captive's chain,
> The Lover's anguish, and the Miser's fear . . .
> I'd rather lose myself with *thee*, and share
> Thine happy indolence, for one short hour,
> Than live of Sensibility the tool
> For endless ages. Oh! her points have pierc'd
> My soul, till, like a sponge, it drinks up woe.
> (*Poems on Various Subjects*, pp. 50, 52)

Unlike her more powerful male counterpart, the iconic shepherdess in *Rural Lyre* remains significantly unnamed. But she refuses to become one of her own sheep. Rather, she will guide the flock, please herself, and relinquish control to no one.

The French Revolution problematized Yearsley's patriotism. In the play *Earl Goodwin* that marks her first publication since the fall of the Bastille, she champions the French Revolution and its pursuit of liberty. The epigraph confirms to the Bristol audience Yearsley's unabashed ardor for revolutionary goals. By 1793, Yearsley's three poems about the guillotined French monarchs sign a severe change. New fury, she contends, and a phantom sense of liberty drive the revolutionaries forward, and victimize the French monarchs. Now Englishness embraces the oppression of Catholic monarchs. Freedom and English values somewhat shift meaning. In the poem about the king of Poland and Loraski, who opts for suicide over enslavement by Russia, Yearsley commends patriotism and resistance against tyranny.

By opening *Rural Lyre* with "Brutus," Yearsley traces Britain's mythological origins; she foregrounds national pride from the very beginning. Later, "The Genius of England" triumphantly supports the victorious navy.

A woman of a deeply serious cast of mind, Yearsley sought a world without division, a perspective rooted in her rural proletarian origins and her sensitivity to division and injustice around the world. She subscribed to a politics of power and resistance long before More "discovered" her creative talent as a poet. Eventually, she denounced war and slavery, and transhistorically championed oppressed twelfth-century English peasants, a class with whom she closely identified.

Despite being "dropped" by her patron and first publisher, she persevered as a writer, her will and sense of independence unquenchable.[43] Then historical events intervened. Despite an early attraction to the principles of the French Revolution, by 1796 she was praising Britain's military feats. Ultimately she portrayed the revolution in negative terms.

"The Indifferent Shepherdess" brings Yearsley full circle from the dedication; she has traveled from a refusal to be fearful "of general approbation" to scorning male desire and control. She will live life as she chooses.

By 1796, the acid edge of Yearsley's anger—whether over Hannah More's discrediting, Eames's defense of cruelty, or slavemasters' atrocities—has diminished. Personal confrontations abate. At that point, she emerges as a patriotic poet who eulogizes the nation's military might, its origins, nature, and family.

With a less gendered orientation than Mary Collier and Mary Scott and a complex class vantage point, Ann Yearsley remained committed to the concept of global union. Her own term was "social love."

Inevitably imaged as a querulous ingrate with oddly remarkable talents and personal initiative, she complicated the politics of gender and class throughout her artistic career. Through refusing class collusion and publicizing her altercation with Hannah More, Ann Yearsley fashioned a subversive multiple identity that was both liminal and culturally acceptable; she wrote a mainstream as well as an alternative discourse. With any means available, she dissolved efforts to erase her art and proudly claimed the right to autonomy and self-construction.

CHAPTER FIVE

Ann Yearsley, the Unpublished Poems: Confrontation Unmediated, Empathy Undisguised

Despite the circumstances that threatened to obscure Ann Years-ley's talents, she pressed on with an impressive body of work. The unpublished poems present yet another set of scenarios on the fear-less young poet. They especially indicate how the alteracation with Hannah More personally troubled Ann Yearsley and how much she strove to keep an evenhanded self-representation afloat before the public. Let me back up.

When the milkwoman-poet from Bristol died in 1806, she left behind a large batch of unpublished poems entitled *Additions to Several Poems*.[1] They were handwritten on blank pages of a first edition of *Poems on Several Occasions*, Yearsley's first volume of verse, that now resides in the Bristol Public Library.

Above the first group of handwritten poems, including "To Stella," Yearsley superscribed this note: "The following lines were composed immediately after Miss H. More's haughty treatment of the Author, Time and Resolution having calmed Resentment in the bosom of the latter, Generosity forbade the publication of several Pieces which were written in these painful moments."[2] Stella was the classical name that Yearsley used for Hannah More in the first volume of poems, a well-known pseudonym for More in the press.

After the Stella group, in chronological order, comes a hand-written thirty-eight-line addition to the printed poem, "Address to Friendship," that appeared in *Poems on Several Occasions* (1785). At the end of these lines, Yearsley adds that they were "written in the Book June 19, 1788 by Mr. Gossip's Grateful and very humble Servant, Ann Yearsley."

After these additional lines appended to "Address to Friendship" is a poem entitled "To Mr. Chetwood"; then follows "To the King: On His Majesty's arrival at Cheltenham 1788." (King George arrived in Cheltenham after June 1788.) Three poems to someone called Horatio come next: their titles are "To Mr G. who declined making himself known to the Author"; "The Answer. By Horatio," dated June 23, 1788; and "On passing the window of Horatio, and seeing Him sitting in a melancholy attitude," dated October 18, 1788. *Additional Poems* ends with three poems: "Sappho Justified either way . . ."; "To Dorinda on hearing her sing in an elegant Circle at Bristol Wells," dated Clifton, August 18, 1789; and lastly "To William Cromartie Yearsley. On his becoming a pupil of Mr. _____." This last poem, addressed to Yearsley's son, turns out to be the only poem to be published out of the handwritten pages.

Ann Yearsley wrote *Additions* while she was preparing her second volume, *Poems on Various Subjects*, and several of her long occasional poems for publication. Except for the tribute to her son, however, she seems to have decided against publishing these particular poems, sometimes for obvious reasons. According to the superscription of "To Stella," Yearsley wrote these sad, angry poems just after the quarrel with her patron and before Yearsley had cooled off. She composed them in that uneasy space between the publication of the first volume that added the irate defense of her interaction with More and the second volume that announced her cultural independence. Had she included "To Stella" in the second volume, it would have dramatically titillated the reading public, since it sharply contrasted with More's recent praise of Yearsley in a private letter to Elizabeth Montagu. This letter was subsequently included as part of the prefatory apparatus to the first volume of Yearsley's poems.[3] Had the eulogy and "To Stella" appeared within two years of each other, Hannah More's public image, class bias, and defensiveness would have become more apparent. Yearsley, on the other hand, would have emerged as an angry yet vulnerable victim who rightfully resented such condescension; she would also have flouted certain common assumptions about gentle womanhood, thus exacerbating charges about her ungratefulness.

In short, Yearsley opted for discretion and published the toned-down version of "To Stella" in the second volume. Entitled "To Those Who Accuse the Author of INGRATITUDE," the poem decries Yearsley's detractors as "low, groveling, and confin'd . . . incapacious souls." She asks them why affliction befalls "the wretch Inured and patient in the pangs of woe?" Her published response, that is, is much more generalized than her *ad feminam* attack in the unpublished "To Stella." By dampening her outrage in the published poem, Yearsley preempts accusations of vituperative excess toward More; she prefers to let her feelings speak for themselves in her matter-of-fact appendix to the fourth edition of the first volume. In that account, she maintains her poise as she reacts, seemingly spontaneously, to injustice.

In "To Those Who Accuse," Yearsley compares herself to "An object, wand'ring from her destin'd course, / Quitting the purer path, where spirit roves, / To sip Mortality's soul-clogging dews, / and Feast on Craft's poor dregs." Scorning opponents for being so distanced from the "bright sublimity of Truth," she applauds singularity and her right to be an artist.[4] Decoded, singularity means a cross between uniqueness and independence. Imbuing her narrator (very little distanced from herself) with a rich and passionate sensibility, she validates volatility, but still presses these emotions into a highly constrained form.

In the unpublished "To Stella," by contrast, written at an emotional peak, perhaps a year earlier than "To Those Who Accuse," Yearsley assails More directly, challenging her patron's moral integrity. The narrator (again a double for Yearsley) authoritatively advises Stella (clearly Hannah More) not to intervene in the lives of people like herself. Yearsley emerges as one who has temporarily lost a personal and political struggle only to embrace a self-imposed exile. To back up her stance as a hapless victim of More's opportunism, Yearsley's testimonies and poems represent More as someone who sought credit for patronizing an "uneducated" poet. On the other hand, More wanted Yearsley to do as she was told. In Yearsley's view, More's actions constituted a double standard that denied Yearsley personal agency. She was displayed, exhibited almost, as a laboring woman who independently composed poems—an artistic "find"—but she was not to be allowed financial autonomy. Yearsley had no choice in the matter and was indirectly instructed to know her place. Reclaiming this rightful place down in the metaphorical "vale," Yearsley warns More not to bait a "darling Idol" (Yearsley herself, we assume) with too much insult or persecution. Otherwise that idol, she warns, will unveil More's hypocrisy.

The narrator insists, too, that she adopt other tactics to offset insults to which she is subjected: "Oh Thou shoulds't weigh the feelings of the Soul!" she exclaims, stressing her vulnerability. She employs multiple stylistic devices and florid tropes to ridicule her opponent.

Stella has robbed the narrator of illusion. Resigned to life at the borders, the narrator can at least be who she wants to be, rather

than submit to Stella's idea of her ontological status. She charges
More with cheating herself and by implication cheating Yearsley as
well:

> . . . while borne on *Principle* she soars
> Yea leaves the Stars behind! alas *thy* wing
> Has long been wearied! in the guileless Chace
> Of a delusive Meteor, form'd to cheat
> Thy Soul, and lure her far from *honest* Candour.

These bold accusations would have shocked the reading public
as well as More's supporters.[5] Intrepidly, Yearsley configures the
virtuous and popular evangelical model woman writer as a figure of
duplicity. In turn, Yearsley would have been imaged as a querulous
ingrate. The unpublished lines in "Stella" suggest one of Yearsley's
dilemmas: What language does the underdog use for denoting a cri-
sis over class relations? What vocabulary, syntax, and mood will
appropriately express "loss, rupture, and [cultural] deterritorializa-
tion"?[6] In the end, Yearsley opts not to indulge and thereby occupies
a slightly less controversial location.

In "Despondence," an unfinished, provocative poem, the narrator voices loneliness. Like Yearsley herself, she mourns the loss of a
mother and patron without directly referring to them. She muses on
suicide as a cure for depression and a sense of abandonment:

> How many gloomy years have silent pass'd
> While each seem'd still more joyless than the last
> My prospect barren,—sympathy unknown
> Eternal Slumber is my cure alone.

In "To Stella," the narrator had already confessed that mental pain,
the dismal prospect of a culturally silent life overwhelmed her. Only
death can transcend such despair. In a Hamlet-like echo, she would
dare the "untry'd Region" of suicide—she admits—only if she were
to understand it better.

In public life, such intimations of suicide would have served
Yearsley ill in spite of the sympathy invoked by her dire straits.
Branded unChristian, she would have been relegated to an even
more ignoble status.

In the assertive lines that follow "To Stella" and "Despondence"—penned informally while Yearsley wrote the emotionally
fraught poems—the author fingers the false friends who surround
her. The lines read as follows: "The Author gives a strong proof that

if she could make her own bargain, She would choose better Company in the next world [her mother rather than More?] than she has in this." Perhaps surprisingly, Yearsley assumes responsibility for her lot.

The handwritten addition to the "Address to Friendship" pursues the argument of "To Stella" and "Despondence"; it recontextualizes Yearsley's preoccupation with friendship. As a poem, "The Address" appears first in 1785 in *Poems on Several Occasions*, then it reappears in *Rural Lyre*, Yearsley's last volume of poems published in 1796. (The handwritten addition shows up only in the 1785 volume.) In both volumes, the poem features friendship as an "immortal essence" that "binds the willing soul." Genuine friendship has no boundaries, although people should exercise caution in searching for it. In Yearsley's views, the relationship is a metaphysical one between souls, not physical persons. Unlike the sentiments in the two printed poems, the handwritten addition to the "Address to Friendship" in 1785 argues that physical want kills friendship, a multifaceted contention in the light of Yearsley's circumstances. Most transparently, poverty permanently separated Yearsley from her mother. Furthermore, Yearsley glosses how her desire for remuneration—another form of physical want—chilled her friendship with More. Death and want are twins to whom Yearsley is, she claims, related. Only her ability to create fosters that sense of equality intrinsic to a well-balanced friendship. In this addition, the narrator is so grief-stricken that she wishes she never had a friend, an impossible concept in the original poem where friendship is solely related to physical environment. Yearsley even contends that the desire for friendship is a morally unworthy act, since want can drive it away.

Like Collier, Yearsley was accentuating the difficulties of exigent daily living. In readers' eyes, her authentic cobbling of death and deprivation would have challenged, maybe cancelled her image as a fierce upstart.

A substantial subset of the unpublished poems that includes the poems about More, personal despondence, and feelings about friendship conjures up a woman who feels so uncertain of her social place and so grievously wronged that she contemplates suicide. Class and gender persistently interlock. Then ideas about nation and Englishness surface.

Almost coincident with this mournful questioning of the possibility of friendship among deprived people, Yearsley pens another unpublished poem that sits oddly with the earlier poems. Entitled "To the King: on His Majesty's arrival at Cheltenham 1788," the poem pays tribute to King George III when he visits Cheltenham to take the waters in 1788: the king's exhaustion and biliousness were common knowledge in the press.[7] Yearsley's royal encomium includes references to her own happy state.

In other words, the same year that she denies the possibility of friendship and ponders economic hardship and suicide, she presents the public with a self-disciplined narrator who is seemingly content: "No *Boon I ask*— blest with a mod'rate store / *Content* is mine— e'en Kings possess no more." To the king she discloses that her undisciplined talent has been "taught to rove thro' simple scenes: Wild, as the tunefull Lark that loves the grove."

Perhaps Yearsley admires the king for his unassuming manner. But why does she keep her grief and sense of injustice to herself? Perhaps she thought of Stephen Duck, her failed relation with Hannah More, and the advantages she might accrue from George III's patronage. His apparent ease as he walks among the people appeals to Yearsley and keenly contrasts with More's supercilious behavior toward laboring-class people:

"Never did schoolboys enjoy their holydays equal to what we have done our little excursion," wrote the Queen to Prince Augustus. . . . The King went about everywhere almost like a plain country gentleman, with no guards and often unaccompanied by equerries.[8] Wraxhall told how he delighted "to enter into conversation with persons who accidentally fell in his way." He chatted with farmers about crops and prices. He considered the textile country around Stroud, then mightily prosperous, the most beautiful sight he had ever seen. The royal party visited the Gloucester Infirmary and the new half-built County Jail, the King leaving £300 for the relief of its debtor inmates. . . . Wherever they went, as the Queen wrote, "immense crowds of people" welcomed them everywhere. The King's popularity was plain for all to see, and he returned to Windsor delighted with his five weeks holiday and apparently quite restored in health.[9]

In the same poem, the narrator eulogizes General James Wolfe, who died in 1777 scaling the heights above Quebec as he secured a colonial victory for the English. General Wolfe's "inspiration," the narrator claims, induces such ardor in bucolic youth that the king—whom she calls a pious pastor—will be proud to rule: "O These are Joys worthy a Monarch's Soul!" Yearsley might also have admired General Wolfe's candor and courage. She wants him to listen to a contented rural muse whose poems could cheer him up: "song can fiercer minds control." By representing herself as a carefree poet, the Yearsley-like narrator dissolves her own fiery demons and elicits public respect; she manifests a version of what was later to be termed negative capability. By acclaiming Wolfe's exploits, Yearsley joins the national consensus—a haven for a marginalized individual.

Next, she underlines her idea of personal harmony by painting a scene of tranquil country living blest by George III. By contrast, she stresses the devastating effect of war on provincial populations, indicting foreign invaders of English shores: "ruthless ravages" reduce the people to want. To peasants she attaches a certain artlessness, almost an insensitivity to the feelings of a monarch. This stance seems notably incongruous alongside Yearsley's usual disregard for arbitrary authority and her utmost respect for class peers. Again the need for patronage might be erupting. *"Their Thoughts* extend no farther than the mead / On which their *Herds*, or harmless *Lambkins*, feed. . . . / Their *Life's* enjoyment being *Three* at most. . . . / They breathe, they eat, they die, in peace unknown / Nor heed the Joys or sorrows of a Throne."

By the next year, as George III exhibits signs of derangement, the regency debate gears up. Beyond that and perhaps more to the point, while Yearsley composes poems for *Rural Lyre* that would appear in 1796, the king opposes the French Revolution, his support for Louis XVI and his opposition to human rights unequivocal. In validating a proslavery stance, the monarch attracts followers away from the abolitionist camp. Psychologically, he helps to turn the emotional tide toward a plantocratic vantage point in postrevolutionary England.

Presumably, these events would have caused Yearsley to reconsider any hope of patronage. She might have deemed it insupportable to eulogize a king who publicized undesirable views. She might have had second thoughts about foregrounding peasant simplicity—the same class-based peasants, after all, are helping to mount a revolution across the English Channel. In 1788, Ann Yearsley had already penned her abolitionist diatribe, "Poem on the Inhumanity of the Slave Trade," that almost coincided with the publication of Hannah More's pro-abolition poem. Given her radical beliefs, Yearsley backed away from apostrophizing George III; distance and principle might have become linked as they did in the case of Hannah More.

The three unpublished poems to Horatio that follow this poem to the monarch similarly invite plural readings. A footnote in the second volume, *Poems on Various Subjects*, provides a clue to Horatio's identity.

Yearsley seems to have written about "Horatio" in a somewhat displaced way in *Poems on Various Subjects*. That volume includes a poem entitled "Elegy, Written on the Banks of the Avon, where the Author took a last Farewel of her Brother." This poem centerstages the speaker's/Yearsley's eulogy to her dead brother but also addresses several other deaths that Yearsley had mourned. These echo the tragic drowning-death circumstances of the Smith family.[10] She opens "Elegy" by eulogizing her own drowned brother:

> O God, what tremors shook
> The strongest pow'rs of my reluctant soul,
> When, from his eyes, I took their farewel gaze. (P. 38)

Several times she chides the "wave," both "false" and "fatal." The speaker then parallels his death with that of sad Maria,/Mary Smith "who in a fit of despair, plunged in the Avon," (p. 38) Mary Collier's sadness about Stephen Duck's suicide by drowning quietly resonates. The narrator assumes a "kind Creator, who in pity strikes,/From thy account, this heav'n-opposed act." (p. 40).

She then describes and eulogizes Mary Smith's brother, Richard—called Horatio in the poem—who drowned while trying to save his own brother from drowning, after his sister Mary had already drowned. Here are "Elegy"'s words on Richard Smith's fatal loving dive:

> In Friendship's strongest act;
> When bearing young Philander to the shore,
> He sigh'd his soul away. Oh! 'twas a scene,
> Where Horror revell'd; on the margin stood
> Horatio,* smiling at the sportive youth,
> Who fain would lash the wave with strengthless arm.
> Ah, effort vain! Down! down! he hopeless sinks:
> While in Horatio's bosom Nature swell'd
> More strong than tempest wild; dauntless he plung'd
> 'Mid liquid death. (P. 41)

The asterisk attached to Horatio's name in the poem refers to the following footnote: "R. Smith, (Brother to Maria) who seeing their younger brother sinking, plung'd into the river with his clothes on; he saved the youth, but was drowned himself" (p. 41). (Curiously enough, Richard Smith cannot be the surgeon of the same name to whom Yearsley addressed a poem in 1788.[11])

Last of all, Yearsley grieves for Richard Smith's son "drowned two years after, near the same place with his father." She calls on the three beleaguered, drowned souls of the Smith family to carry her feelings to her brother, "thou long-lov'd youth" (p. 42).

In the unpublished poems to Horatio, written later than the second volume of poems in which Horatio/Richard Smith explicitly appears, Yearsley/the speaker amplifies Horatio's grief.[12] In the first unpublished poem, the narrator initially chides Horatio for bottling up sorrow. In the second poem, however, purportedly written by Horatio himself, he instructs the narrator to stop intruding on his grief, a doubled signification, given Ann Yearsley's immersion in maternal mourning.

In the third poem, "On passing the window of Horatio, and seeing Him sitting in a melancholy attitude," Ann Yearsley again encodes memory as "relentless." She objects to the fact that neither balm, opiate, nor "strong philosophy" can dissipate Horatio's melancholy. Stanza three specifically echoes a death by drowning, like Richard Smith's sister's in the Avon:

> Alas I fear not! for thy wounds are deep
> As Ocean's bed, where horrors live unseen
> In secret pomp, thy mourning Soul would weep
> Lest vulgar noise, profane her sacred scene.

From there Ann Yearsley moves to personalize Horatio's/Richard Smith's tragedy, now explicitly reminding readers that when she was mourning her mother, personal detractors refused to leave her in peace:

> Oh the blasting breath
> Of many-ey'd Opinion, taints the air,
> Her Fiends torment the guiltless e'en in death
> And drop their venom, on the senseless Bier.

She comforts Horatio by reminding him that dwelling on sadness is not cowardly. At the same time, she urges him to rally as best he can: "The *brave* will struggle long,—*Fools* soon dispair." Time will heal, she reminds him; taking hold of his child will comfort him and help friends who seek to help Horatio:

> Ah take the Cherub to thy frozen breast
> She'll health, and strength, and vital warmth impart

Make Those who *love Thee* for thy Virtues, *blest*
By giving Joy to thy afflicted heart.

Yearsley's exclusion of the poems from publication invites a
number of speculations. At the very least, Yearsley might have opted
to close the shutters on family tragedy.[13]

Nonetheless, Horatio's poems throw light on the narrator's
(Yearsley's) personality, the slippage between author and speaker
that the title invites. She is determined to comfort the mourner, then
highlights the mourner's complaint about intrusiveness.

What could Yearsley be saying, we wonder, about her own ability to grieve for her mother? Were people invasive? Does she regret
her versified public announcement of her grief? Perhaps the Horatio
poems demanded too much "reliving" on Yearsley's part. Would she
have shelved them before Horatio's own accidental death—let's
say—because they were too painful to publish? Imbricated in the
Horatio poems are possible allusions to Yearsley's own life.

On a related note, Yearsley's seemingly whimsical quatrain on
being censured by her mother and brother when she was a girl,
"Extempore," reveals that she has left the most intense period of
mourning behind:

Dame Nature hath sent me a knave for a Brother
A surly vexatious and lunatic Mother
Were these sent to Egypt as Scourges for Vice
What need then of Locust, of Frogs, Fleas, or Lice?

She can now afford to pen an almost light-hearted ditty that projects
female adolescent contempt for her mother and a male sibling. The
quatrain suggests a flippant side—or even a brutally honest, irate
side. On the other hand, the nonpublication of "Extempore" suggests
that these gentle observations neither fitted her mid-1790s mood nor
her public image. The juxtaposition of grief and persiflage was more
than she wanted. Or perhaps she needed to resolve a memory, to exor-
cize the anger she felt at her mother's needless death a decade earlier,
in a symbolic reworking of the past. The "I" of earlier times "is constituted in relation to the "I" of the locutor.[14] The personal tragedy
of the Smiths—it seems—might have induced a change of perspective.

The second short extemporaneous single-stanza polemic also
curses the effect of greed. It obliquely reindicts More for trying to
expropriate Yearsley's earnings and anchors the importance of economics in Yearsley's life. Although the narrator's presence in the
stock exchange is never explained, she constructs the visit as casual;

"writing to the moment," she jotted down the lines with a pencil while she was there. A plurality of meanings opens up. Yearsley could have been negotiating for the sale of property from her circulating library and wandered in to see how men of substance conducted themselves—she knew she would soon be nudging into the bottom levels of that class. Since her second patron was the Earl of Bristol, she was becoming acquainted with Bristolians who frequented financial institutions. But the visit (if such a visit took place) was not worthy of pursuit or inclusion. That much is clear.

The penultimate unpublished poem that Yearsley composed, "Sappho, Justified, either way," outlines a crucial component of her philosophical beliefs. She debates free will versus predetermination, referred to as "Cause" in the poem. If there is no free will, she argues, virtue is nonexistent; in fact, the very idea of virtue is fatuous. People cannot receive credit for being "themselves" because everything is predetermined. The concepts of good and evil lose their meaning. Rejecting this idea of a prime mover fixing the universe irreversibly, she claims to exercise choice, to be able in certain ways to pursue Truth and God: "We're Rogues, Thieves, Lawyers, Hangmen, Priests, or Knaves / And each by turns, the other, hangs and saves / By this same Rule of Cause;—well, be it so!" Yearsley believes that she is justified as a poet, regardless, but if life is a choice, then her role as a poet is partly of her own making.

A fascinating poem in its deliberations, "Sappho, Justified" stages a debate that Yearsley inevitably deemed unwise to publicize. Perhaps she could have been accused of attacking evangelical beliefs—the ideas of the Clapham Sect—to which More subscribed. In terms of philosophical commitment to free will, Yearsley might be "digging" at Hannah More for her firm religious views that Yearsley does not share. But unlike More, whose belief system operates within well-defined parameters, Yearsley is less sectarian. The fluid notion that people might or might not have choice infuriates Yearsley. In the 1787 volume, Yearsley had already wrestled with these conceptualizations. In "The Materialist," the narrator upbraids those who deny human beings the possibility of metaphysical life, who attempt to describe "the natural processes and human experience in terms of arrangements and rearrangements of changeless atoms, or indivisible material particles, in empty space."[15] According to this analysis, atoms alone exist. Consequently the world results from chance: mechanistic causes explain all phenomena as well as spirituality, ethics, and morals. Senses have no access to truth or knowledge, nor does the intellectual life exist outside of a mechanistic explanation. Spirituality amounts to superstition.[16]

Then a key appears. Yearsley denounces the materialist as a "vile ravager of order," a falsely moral individual who boasts of "virtues which exist without a cause." Most strikingly, Yearsley disdains the fact that materialists have nothing to live for since they eschew the afterlife: "Vain the web / Hoary Philosophy shall ever spin / If, in thy future views, thou ne'er canst form/Some *good* to hope for!"

In other words, "Sappho, Justified" and "The Materialist" doubly underline Yearsley's love of social order and her dislike—also articulated in the later antiwar poems—of general unruliness. This insecurity makes her balk at a philosophy that threatens her belief system and a desire for harmony:

If of these Elements, weak Man's combin'd
Are all his actions, by his *Will* confin'd?
And if not ruled by *Will*, You'll say *some Cause*
More old, and *Self-Existent* gives him Laws;
The question *is*: if He hath *Will* or *not*?
Whether, with Freedom acting, or by Lot?
If freely, Motion, in him freely moves,
And NO first self-existent Spirit, proves.
Again, if a First-cause, doth motion give
No will in secondary-beings live.

At another level, it also contradicts what is for Yearsley the definition and joy of art. Thus "Thee" at the end of "Sappho, Justified" in the lines below at one level signifies Sappho herself. Sappho constitutes and is defined as commitment to poetry and to art—"But own my Soul, moves in a pure degree / And Boasts her Freedom, in pursuing *Thee*." Yearsley's decision not to link her atomist views with art inscribes an intellectual—usually concealed—nervousness.

The last poem to appear in "Additional Poems" is "To William Cromartie Yearsley. On his becoming a pupil of Mr._____". Ostensibly an apostrophe to her son William, Yearsley deemed that poem alone suitable for publication.[17] Highlighting a host of thematics— maternal and social love, virtue, reason, duplicity, and selfishness— it raises the vexed question of sexual politics. Beyond that, Yearsley makes distinct changes from the unpublished poem to the printed text. Most telling is the switch from two lines that deride a woman made boastful by mistreatment of men. "The Brave ne'er own a wretch Who dares to boast / Beauty thus wreck'd on bleak affliction's coast." The unpublished version tenders no sympathy to this woman and interjects negative reactions to her behavior; in the printed version Yearsley substantially softens this attack.

Woman, from false tuition, false pretence,
Like some stray'd infant ever seeks defence;
And oft in search of peace, the victim proves
Serious destruction with the Man she loves. (P. 23)

Having exhibited compassion for the abuse women suffer Yearsley also reaffirms her commitment to the concept of social love that she extolled in her antislavery poem. She clarifies that national and domestic harmony matters to her in the last line of the filial apostrophe: "And thy fair brow be crown'd by social love."[18] Occupying a transitional space among Yearsley's works, the republished poem interweaves the personal and political and draws away from explicit evaluations of historical events. It positively foregrounds Yearsley's status as a mother—a role that would appeal to the public.

Between her first and last volume of poems, from 1785 to 1796, Yearsley published the poem opposing the slave trade and *Stanzas of Woe* (1790), as well as the poem to her son William.[19]

Rural Lyre includes the aforementioned "Address on Friendship: A Fragment," slightly modified from the version in the 1785 volume. To the 1796 "Address," Yearsley appends a seventeen-line parenthesis that ostensibly explains the republication. Unspoken, however, is the fact that by republishing this poem, Yearsley resurrects the quarrel with Hannah More, the matter, as it were, that rendered her a celebrity. She refuses to allow Hannah More an unsullied reputation as a "champion of the oppressed." By 1796, More's published tales and Yearsley's poems had brought fame to both women. Hence this third volume would have been a "natural home" for the earlier unpublished poems. But times had changed. The poems of *Rural Lyre*, articulating Yearsley's response to the revolutionary epoch, breathed in a different political, psychological, and cultural space. No metaphorical room was available for a letter-inverse from a courtesy book ("To Mr. Chetwood") or a weakly formulated tribute to a Bristol singer ("To Dorinda") and three personal poems to and about a certain Horatio. The only poem she published from this group was the poem to William that inscribed social love, a concept consistent with French revolutionary aims of worldwide global harmony. The poem marks Yearsley's radical-global shift, first outlined in her poem against the slave trade. Yearsley continues to address local issues occasionally—she berates the mayor of Bristol in *Stanzas of Woe* (1790) for his treatment of her children—but her private life becomes less a matter of public record, less a personal staging.

Yearsley's decision about what to publish seems unconnected to self-representation. She shied from appearing as a vituperative, vulnerable laboring-class subject who either acted on the spur of the moment or indulged in morally shocking meditations. She would be less volatile but she would always act out of a sense of justice. That representation she never surrendered. Operating on several registers, the poems also reveal how resentful Hannah More was and how she tried to limit Yearsley's possibilities and Yearsley's creativity.

The unpublished poems shake loose some indeterminacy attached to poems in earlier volumes. For example, they contextualize Yearsley's views of Chatterton and suicide, and her own feelings of despair. They also highlight Yearsley's refinement, her self-discipline in deciding against publication. Hannah More had unwittingly instructed Yearsley about the peril of impetuousness and the value of second thoughts.

Yearsley's unpublished poems stress her commitment to the status quo, social order, and friendship. Human bonding is the personal face of political harmony, the private interaction that connects people worldwide. For the most part, Yearsley's quest for justice renders her poems highly controversial.

First, she launches a burning attack on More. On a related note, she indicts false friendship, with mordant remarks about hypocrisy. Further, she philosophically favors choice and free will, running in the face of Hannah More's "fixed" evangelical beliefs. Put another way, the unpublished poems chronicle the fact that Yearsley's public image troubles her. So she adds nothing to fan the flames of controversy. On the other hand, she does have her limits. In *Rural Lyre*, she enthusiastically supports British opposition to the French Revolution while her unpublished tribute to George III condemns war and underwrites a complacent peasantry. Perhaps she wanted to eschew certain jejune contentions regarding peasants' ignorance about the humanity of royalty; sovereigns also suffer pain. At any rate, *Additional Poems* exemplifies cultural struggle and sheds new light on Ann Yearsley's art and beliefs. The manuscript mediates the notorious public profile of Yearsley that was circulated from 1786 to 1789, the momentous years of her creative life.

Ann Yearsley writes these unpublished poems early in her artistic career, before the storming of the Bastille. Loosely speaking, they divide into two batches, one personal, the other political. The personal poems themselves divide up: they feature an appalled Yearsley, bespeaking an anger born of insecurity and damaged feelings. The poems on Richard Smith confirm her altruism, her sensitivity toward others' sadness. The Horatio poems explain her generosity to those who befriend her. Forced to suppress so much, at some level she internalizes that she is undeserving. Thus loving attention thrills her.[20]

The political poems are another matter. Yearsley's unmediated patriotism and love for the royal pair echoes Mary Collier's. Like Collier, Yearsley feels the frailty of her class position; engaging in a politics of class and gender identity, she knows, is a risky business.

Besides, Yearsley does not overtly acknowledge her running battle as a former milkwoman who was determined to be recognized as an artist. Hence, her volumes of poetry betray a certain indeterminacy, a refusal to be essentialized. Her poems sign the angst of crises and rupture while underlining love as the base of all communication. But these tensions convey a pervasive and ultimately unresolved textual worry about being too strong versus not being strong enough. Sometimes she seems ambivalent about her own position on the borders, about identifying the "other."

In that sense, her identity is kaleidoscopic, her texts so frankly unapologetic and oppositional that they become manifestoes of a hidden class unease, of a bravado that cannot cover up the denunciations it wants to drown out.[21]

Disallowing dependency, Ann Yearsley keeps her poems on a raw edge, as ongoing sites of contention like herself. Without articulating it as such, Yearsley was engaged in a cultural politics of identity, an effort to make her mark as a laboring-class woman whom class superiors considered unworthy. Gradually, she plays out her anti-authoritarian ethic within a global context, eventually inflecting it with a safe patriotism. This happens only after a personally and professionally perilous early affiliation with the French Revolution.

The circumstances of Ann Yearsley's death to this date are like the circumstances of her early life, obscure and finally unknown. After *Rural Lyre*, Yearsley withdrew from the cultural stage, reconsumed by family affairs: a beloved son died in 1799, her husband in 1803. An inhabitant of Melksham in Wiltshire, where Yearsley probably spent her last years, recorded that "Ann Yearsley was never seen, except when she took her solitary walk, in the dusk of the evening."[22] Not until the end of her life did she lapse into the very twilight in which detractors had sought to cast her at the start of her auspicious career.

CHAPTER SIX

Janet Little, the Ayrshire Dairywoman: Gender, Class, and Scottish National Identity

Concurrently with Ann Yearsley, Scotswoman Janet Little uses her volume of poems to protect a complex class and cultural perspective and a controversial nationalist position. Little, furthermore, applauds the talents of ploughman-poet Robert Burns, as Mary Collier extols thresher-poet Stephen Duck. Similarly, Little's personal feelings for Burns complicate her text. Collier, Yearsley, and Little collectively uphold a positive laboring-class identity with a strong accompanying sense of cultural location.

Nonetheless, as a Scottish poet and laboring woman, Janet Little writes poems that frequently function as gendered, anticolonial testimonials. Unlike Collier, Yearsley, and Scott who privilege English liberty as a crucial tenet, Little underscores a Scottish nationalist vantage point and celebrates its warrior-heroes. Within this group of poets, Englishness and Scottishness are oppositional terrains that contest for cultural dominance. Put slightly differently, Little still remains in a colonial relationship with Collier, Yearsley, and Scott, despite class alliances.

Besides, Janet Little is prepared to struggle for acceptance as an artist and for a chance to display her abilities. In a transcendent sense, like Collier and Yearsley she forges a historical recovery of women poets, representing an alternate viewpoint. She marks her poems with the signs of a revolutionary era and a laboring woman in fraught and ultimately irreconcilable cultural locations.

Like her laboring-class predecessors who aim to enter the public arena of letters, Janet Little, the "Scotch milkmaid" who published a volume of poems in 1792, embeds her poems with multiple messages and concerns, some overt, others submerged. Commendatory tributes to Robert Burns enhance her own cultural standing while she extends mandated politeness to patrons and employers from the middle class and gentry. At the same time, Little questions Burns's relationship with women by obliquely critiquing power-based gender relations in his seemingly benign conventional lyrics and poems.[1] Her politic of class, national, and gendered identity, moreover, directly relates to her background.

Born in 1759, the same year as Robert Burns, Janet Little was the daughter of George Little, a hired farm laborer or cottar in Nether Bogside, near Ecclefechan in Dumfriesshire, Scotland.[2] After a short time in service, she was hired by the Reverend Johnstone and remained in his household for several years as a family servant. She began writing poems during this time. Subsequently, as a chambermaid or "bairn's-woman" or dry nurse, she entered the service of Frances Dunlop of Dunlop, her patron-cum-employer, who was also a patron and correspondent of Robert Burns. Energetically encouraged by Mrs. Dunlop, Janet Little wrote poems at Dunlop House.[3] Dunlop continued to act as an informal patron after Little left her service sometime after 1786 to become a child's nurse and eventually superintendent of the dairy at Loudoun Castle in Ayrshire, which had been leased by Dunlop's daughter, Susan, after the death of the earl of Loudoun.[4] The earl was also the father of the young countess to whom Little was to dedicate her volume of poems.[5] This position as dairy superintendent was highly valued for its financial security, in a decade when, "even before 1786, 7,000 families had emigrated from the Lowlands, mainly from the Borders" where Little grew up."[6] As a result of this occupation and the publication of her poems, Janet Little became popularly known as "the Scotch milkmaid," a cognomen that appeared on the title page of her volume of poems published in 1792.[7]

At that time, Scottish laboring-class poets enjoyed a wide audience, of working- and middle-class people as well as gentry like Frances Dunlop; their poems were much in demand. Especially renowned in Scotland, Robert Burns was invariably called "the ploughman poet."[8]

Janet Little dedicated her volume of poems to twelve-year-old Flora Mure Campbell, Countess of Loudoun.[9] She was acting on the advice of James Boswell, to whom Little wrote inquiring if he would consent to be her dedicatee.[10] Boswell shrewdly recommended that Little ask the countess. The countess was born in August 1780. Succeeding her father at the age of six after his suicide in 1786, she was entrusted to the care of the earl and countess of Dumfries, with whom she resided in Dumfries until the death of the earl in 1803. The power of the countess of Loudoun's name, Robert Burns's assistance in filling up the subscription bill, and Frances Dunlop's vigorous drumming up of takers attracted about seven hundred subscriptions, the countess herself purchasing twelve copies, Dunlop and her relatives twenty copies. The dedication reads as follows: "To the Right Honourable Flora, Countess of Loudoun. The following Poems are with Permission, Humbly Inscribed, by Your Ladyship's Ever Grateful, and Obedient, Humble Servant, Janet Little."

Reaffirming a desire implied in the dedication to be accepted by potential patrons, employers, and their friends, Little opens with a tribute to the countess that precedes the text proper: it first delineates the aristocrat's superior class position and the conduciveness of Loudoun Castle to art and joy: "Will gentle Loudoun deign to lend an ear," and "Within your walls my happiness I found . . . Luxuriant flourish, like the plants around: / Blithe as the birds . . . I pour'd the willing lay" (p. 25). The speaker rejoices (she claims) in her situation at the castle, as well as the charity and lessons in virtue that the aristocrats extend to the aged and rural poor: "ev'ry comfort rural life affords" (p. 26). She enjoys herself so much, she writes, "My life in careless ease might run, / My age supported by my master's son." Somewhat ambiguously, with a self-satisfying whisper, she contrasts the immortality of her humble lines with the laying to rest in the earth of "honor'd Patrons" (p. 25). Sadness further reigns in the household because a child has died—possibly she refers here to the death of Susan Dunlop's first child. Only the speaker's "sad verse" can "grant that shelter" which the "good and great" can no longer tender (p. 27). Although Little apologizes for the anguish her lines arouse, she again intimates that her verse is, by contrast, immortal.

Little follows the dedication and commendatory poem with one additional tribute to the countess's family and estate. That aside, she utters nothing more in their praise. Instead, references abound to poverty, woe, the toughness of laboring women, and the reality of castle living, albeit implicitly rendered. Her poem on Janet Nicol, "A Poem on Contentment," is a case in point. Its subtitle reads "Inscribed To Janet Nicol, A Poor Old Wandering Woman, Who Lives By the Wall At Loudoun and Used Sometimes To Be Visited By the Countess." Little congratulates Janet Nicol since she is neither a writer nor a person crossed in love. Instead she wishes that

> . . . blithly may ilk neighbour greet you;
> May cakes, and scones, and kibbocks meet you;
> And may they weel ilk pocket cram,
> And in your bottle slip a dram.
> May your wee glass, your pipe and specks,

Be ay preserv'd frae doleful wrecks.
May your wee house, baith snug and warm,
Be safe frae ev'ry rude alarm. (P. 177)

Nicol need not worry, says Little, for the aristocrat will always pro-
vide for her, but does she believe that artificial protection is guaranteed? "For age and want, and wo provides / And over misery presides" (p. 178).

Ventriloquizing through such poignant remarks concerning
Nicol, Little complicates the question of contentment by inscribing it
in class and gender terms. Little also gracefully acknowledges
Frances Dunlop in later poems: one is entitled "To a Lady, A Patron-
ess of the Muses, on Her Recovery from Sickness," the other eulogizes one of Scotland's national heroes, victor of the famous battle at
Stirling Bridge in 1286, William Wallace, Dunlop's ancestor. Its title
is "Verses. Written on a foreigner's visiting the grave of a Swiss gentleman, buried among the descendants of Sir William Wallace,
guardian of Scotland in the thirteenth century."

Configured as commendations to altruistic benefactors, Little's
poems of praise comprise standard appeals to patrons who can facilitate the cultural ascent of a socially disadvantaged woman. Yet
problematizing their patronage is a collective fear by the conservative bourgeoisie and the aristocracy of republican values popularly
subscribed to by the Scottish peasantry and urban workers. The
French Revolution inspired working people by 1791 to assert themselves:

> Burns' sympathy for the old Scots royal house which had won
> independence from England, his national pride, his hatred of
> tyranny, and his enthusiasm for the Rights of Man and for the
> Promise of Liberty, Equality, and Fraternity offered by the
> French Revolution then developing—all form a persuasive
> sequence. *Scots What Hae* is its ringing statement, particularly
> stanzas Five and Six, and a noble prelude [in 1794] to the
> Jacobin cry, "A man's a man for a' that."[11]

Burns's venerated class-leveling song "Scots Wha' Have" (1795)
struck no common chord among sympathizers of the old regime who
pronounced rank more than "the guinea's stamp."[12] Frances Dunlop
stopped corresponding with Burns for eighteen months after he
made light of the royal guillotinings in France. The French Revolution fostered a "police atmosphere" in Scotland.[13]

Despite Burns's prorevolutionary sympathies, however, Mrs. Dunlop and he remained friends, during which time she recommends Janet Little to Burns's attention, dubbing her the "rustic poetess."[14] As a socially well-connected woman who was also related to the heroic Wallace, Frances Dunlop had mixed feelings about Burns's politics; certainly her admiration for the honor he brought to Scotland was unalloyed. The fact that Little pays tribute to Wallace connects Burns and Little as permanent supporters of the nationalist cause. In a letter to Burns, Mrs. Dunlop tells him how reluctantly she allowed Little to leave her service: "thinking a child's maid [for her own daughter, Susan] if she was fit for it, a better place than I had to offer. She was glad to go to Loudoun, because she heard you lived near it, and, as she told me, hoped to see you."[15] The "poetical mania" of the period, as well as Burns's fame after the publication of the Kilmarnock edition of his poems in 1786, also affected the response to Little's volume.[16] Laboring-class poets had become voguish. Burns's editions inspired "a host of shoddy imitators . . . much . . . in tribute to him."[17] Burns even complained about the "servility of my plebeian brethren."[18]

Also in 1789, Little wrote a cordial poem and letter of self-introduction to Burns, exhorting him to peruse her poems; he is a fellow laborer who should favor his own: "I felt a partiality for the author, which I should not have experienced had you been in a more dignified station . . . I shall, in hope of your future friendship, take the liberty to transcribe them."[19] Someone like Janet Little, even lower in the class scale than Burns—her father was a hired laborer, his was a tenant farmer—would have appreciated Burns's struggle to become recognized as a poet. His life was one of "thwarted progress as well as of sturdy rooted vitality."[20] Although limited publications appeared before the 1720s beyond "newspapers, schoolbooks, law papers, and Church pamphleteering,"[21] by midcentury the Enlightenment was emerging "in full vigour."[22] Two years before Burns's book, David Hume commented that Scots were "the People most distinguish'd for Literature in Europe."[23]

In "An Epistle to Mr. Robert Burns," Little updates the distinguished lineage of Scottish culture that ran through Allan Ramsay, one of the recognized champions of vernacular poetry.[24] In constituting Burns as its new embodiment, she renders the issue of Scottishness and national identity paramount. Here she distinctly diverges from her English counterparts, both laboring class like Collier and Yearsley and middle class like Mary Scott. Little eulogizes Burns's ability to captivate a cross-class audience and lavishly lauds his surpassing nature poems: "To hear thy song, all ranks desire; / Sae well thou strik'st the dormant lyre" (p. 161). She also singles out Burns's dedication to Gavin Hamilton: "In unco' bonny, hamespun speech" (p. 161) in order to mock the fulsome dedications of "servile bards wha fawn an' fleech, / Like beggar's messin" (p. 161). These lines contest her exuberant dedication to the young countess. She commends Burns's nature poems, and adds, probably in reference to his poem in praise of "Scotch Drink" and his "Earnest Cry and Prayer": "An' weel ye praise the whiskey gill." No matter how blunt her own quill might become in extolling him, these compliments, she insists, will be accorded him "frae ilka hill" (p. 162). All she can do, she humbly confesses, is "blot thy brilliant shine" with her "rude, unpolish'd strokes" (p. 163).

Burns replies politely but unforthcomingly about this poem; he uses his allegedly untutored social manners to excuse his lack of response. He writes to Dunlop:

> I had some time ago an epistle, part poetic and part prosaic, from your poetess, Mrs. J. L. _____, a very ingenious but modest composition. I should have written her, as she requested, but for the hurry of this new business. I have heard of her and her compositions in this country; and, I am happy to add, always to the honour of her character. The fact is, I know not well how to write to her: I should sit down to a sheet of paper that I knew not how to stain. I am no dab at fine-drawn letter-writing.[25]

With patriotic spirit, Little pays further tribute to Burns by speculating how English men of letters envy his poetic genius. She maps an English tradition with Joseph Addison, Alexander Pope, and Samuel Johnson, who feel jealousy toward "the plough-boy [who sings,] wi' throat sae clear, / They, in a rage, / Their works wad a' in pieces tear / An' curse your page" (p. 162). Instead of more panegyrics, she will pray for all mortals to dispense blessings "with an indulgent care / To Robert Burns" (p. 163).

Inscribing a keener nationalist sentiment, Little foregrounds her gratitude to Burns for bringing honor to Scotland in a poem entitled "Given to a Lady Who Asked Me to Write a Poem." After listing those who "got near [Parnassus's] top: that little fellow Pope, Homer, Swift, Thomson, Addison, an' Young,"[26] she then opts for writing in Scots after stating that Samuel Johnson showed them all up:

> But Doctor Johnson, in a rage,
> Unto posterity did shew
> Their blunders great, their beauties few.

But now he's dead, we weel may ken;
For ilka dunce maun hae a pen,
To write in hamely, uncouth rhymes;
An' yet forsooth they please the times. (P. 114)[27]

Ridiculing Johnson to avenge his critique of Scottish society, she denotes Burns as an overreacher "sous[ing] his sonnets on the court." Here Little uses a concrete image for her activities as a domestic servant. In addition to its meaning of "pouring," *souse* also means sloshing from a pail or a bucket. Forceful associations from the dialect sense of *souse*, meaning to strike a blow, may also bear on the meaning. Then she reverses the initial negative reaction: if Johnson were alive, she protests self-mockingly, he would have gleaned capital for another anti-Scottish Dunciad:

An' what is strange, they praise him for 't.
Even folks, wha're of the highest station,
Ca' him the glory of our nation.
    But what is more surprising still,
A milkmaid must tak up her quill;
An' she will write, shame fa' the rabble!
That think to please wi' ilka bawble.
They may thank heav'n, auld Sam's asleep:
For could he ance but get a peep,
He, wi' a vengeance wad them sen'
A' headlong to the dunces' den. (P. 114)

Unlike Burns, she concludes, a "rustic country queen" like herself has no such versatility; her self-parody turns itself inside out. Through her use of "queen," a common word for "girl" in northeast Scots, Little refers to the debate over writing in Scots. She challenges the alleged inferiority of the vernacular, the idea of measuring up to correct English usage, or "pernicious Anglicizing."[28] Her detachment from Burns only enhances their connections and Burns himself as her reference point, while her choice of "wise" affirms female capacity:

Does she, poor silly thing, pretend
The manners of our age to mend?
Mad as we are, we're wise enough
Still to despise sic paultry stuff. (P. 115)

Burns's talent, she affirms, is to please "a' denominations," instruct people in love, set forth deft though pithy political commentary, and intimidate critics.

Here Little mocks some of the heroes of Collier, Scott, and Yearsley: M. B. explains why Mary Collier has read so little; Mary Scott draws on more obscure figures from the canon because her subject matter—praiseworthy female writers—is audacious; Hannah More boasts that Yearsley had read Milton and Young.

In turn, Little reminds readers that Scottish differs from English and that English is not synonymous with British. She affirms that writing in Scots is a venerable practice at a time when Britain is sharply contesting identitarian politics abroad, when nationalist identity and social politics at a comparative national level were passionately debated. Little raises the question of the English universalizing of British culture, of nationalist, totalizing tendencies. She insists on the separation and worth of Scotland. Her poems are deliberately provocative in this age of "runaway Scottophobia."[29] Attitudes about the relations of men and women in Scotland, traditionally patriarchally oriented, would also have contaminated Little's reception, however patriotic. The question of female manners was a thorny national issue, especially in growing urban centers.[30] Little's social position as a trusted dairywoman on a large estate—as well as her patrons—encouraged her independent spirit. Little also raises the question of her relationship to Burns as a poet and his status (and her own) in the hard-won world of letters.

Little wrote a second poem about Burns, entitled "On a Visit to Mr. Burns," when she traveled to meet him at Ellisland in Dumfriesshire, near where she was born, a visit negotiated through Dunlop's good offices. Unfortunately, she arrived on an inauspicious day when Burns had fallen off his horse—named Pegasus in the poem.[31] She reels from her good fortune in meeting Scotland's top-ranked contemporary poet: "Is't true? or does some magic spell / My wond'ring eyes beguile? / Is this the place where deigns to dwell / The honour of our isle?" (p. 111). Now in his presence, she coyly asserts, he is no longer "bequeath[ing] her a poignant dart" (p. 112). She deplores his present injured condition with a reminder that human life meshes joy and sorrow. She dialogizes some dependence on Burns, perhaps some fear of his cultural power.

In "To My Aunty," a poem in a different vein, the speaker recalls a dream in which critics pounce on her widely published poems for alleged imperfections. Although the critics' debate is not gender-specific, the speaker asserts the vulnerability of all poets, Little herself included. The poem quietly urges Burns to assist her career while remarks arise about Burns's "characteristic touchiness and pride."[32]

In the poem, Tom Touchy is the iconic critical figure whom all other critics desire to please and perhaps emulate. If he wants a line scratched out, they do so. No one—Jack Tim'rous is the example given—wants to oppose this "foremost man": "So much he fear'd a brother's scorn, / The whole escap'd his claws untorn" (p. 166). When James Easy whispers that he likes the poem, Touchy denounces him abusively—at which point the speaker awakes. In her always precarious position as a servant and a female poet, Little takes comfort in commending Burns indirectly and echoing inequitable cultural relationships.

An added irony was Dunlop's fury at Burns's harsh criticisms after Burns's four-day visit to Dunlop, during which they discussed Little's poems in December 1792:

> How did I upbraid my own conceited folly at that instant [affirms Dunlop] that had ever subjected one of mine to so haughty an imperious critic! I never liked so little in my life as at that moment the man whom at all others I delighted to honour. . . . I then felt for Mrs. Richmond (Jenny Little), for you [Burns], and for myself, and not one of the sensations were such as I would wish to cherish in remembrance.[33]

Little's veiled disappointment at Burns's ambivalence notwithstanding, seeming tributes to aristocratic generosity stamp her poems. In contrast to the dedicatory poem eulogizing the countess, the first poem in the volume, "To Hope," denotes the world as a "scene of dole and care." The narrator's self-representation is conflicted, as if she started off intending to placate at least the conservative wing of the reading public and her Tory patron only to be consumed with repressed anger.

At a general level, she discerns disappointment everywhere. Anguish saturates the poem, not least when the speaker proclaims that hope's favor "shall ever / alleviate my wo" (p. 28). Hope illuminates our "dark and dreary way, . . . bend[s] our steps to heav'n, [and] stem[s] the trickling tear." Hope, too, "decorates the chain" of marriage. Though illusory, "we all thy flatt'ring tales believe, / Enamour'd of thy art" (p. 30). She ends by focusing on the power of hope to cancel the terror of death—almost as a cover-up—and on a realistic view of an unhappy world.

Little's need to contain her discontent when she applauds aristocratic generosity is matched by a certain disquiet about Burns that

she likewise has to suppress. In "On Happiness," which foregrounds
her values, she marshals a discourse against the character of the lib-
ertine. She was, after all, a respected member of a Dissenting congregation in Galston, a few miles from Mauchline where Burns
attended an old light (auld licht) Calvinist church. Her respected job
as a dairywoman entailed growing responsibilities as Ayrshire's reputation for cheese grew.[34] The minister the Reverend Mr. Blackwood
described her as a woman of "excellent judgment" who "appreci-
ate[d] something more than mere declamation in a preacher."[35] In
the poem, Little characterizes religion as that institution whose
"force alone can soothe the anxious beast." Her desires, she confides,
are "centre'd all on Him"; (p. 35).[36]

    Like the drunkard in the poem, the libertine never knows hap-
piness, but only "cruel disappointment's rage, / Remorse, despair, the
inmates of his soul" (p. 34). Toward the close of her litany about people
whose lives preclude joy, Little mentions lovers who feed on illusion
and married couples beset by a "thousand ills . . . and . . . bitterness
& wo" (p. 35). This conglomeration of people seems to concur that "Suc-
cessless is the search;/to nobler objects henceforth bend your view"
(p. 35). Interjecting a personal viewpoint, the speaker (Little herself)
observes that only divine law brings "content and calm serenity" to
her "humble station." Her disdain for irreverent, licentious class superiors flashes throughout.

    Little's poems allude to contemporary events in Ayrshire.
Between June and August of 1786, the Mauchline Kirk Session, to
which Burns belonged, rebuked him for fornication; public chiding
was a time-honored practice in the Sunday church service. Burns
had persistently challenged Scottish religious practices with a "common-sense humanitarianism" that stressed salvation by good
works.[37] He deplored the kirk's authority over the people.[38] After
being censured for getting Elizabeth Paton pregnant,[39] Burns
penned a poem to celebrate the birth, defiantly entitling it "Welcome
to a Bastard Wean."[40]

    But despite abhorring Burns's modus operandi toward women,
Little still shies from a direct asssault on Scotland's new standard-
bearer. Striving to raise questions about Burns's way of life, Little
confines her resentment to nuance and allusion. For one thing, she
dialogizes Burns's making free with women—as Little would see it—
by voicing women from another era denouncing men like Burns.[41]
She intertextualizes Burns's actions through displaying the negative experiences of vulnerable women in pastoral verse; penning
slant addresses to Burns, she subtly reminds readers of his conduct
toward women. Echoing Little's internalized conflict is a poem that

contrasts Elizabeth Rowe, the early eighteenth-century English poet known for her piety, with the outspoken Lady Mary Wortley Montagu:

> As Venus by night, so Montague [sic] bright
> Long in the gay circle did shine:
> She tun'd well the lyre, mankind did admire;
> They prais'd, and they call'd her divine. (P. 153)

So pure was Rowe, Little argues, that national morality altered:

> O excellent Rowe, much Britain does owe
> To what you've ingen'ously penn'd:
> Of virtue and wit, the model you've hit;
> Who reads must you ever commend.
>
> Would ladies pursue, the paths trod by you,
> And jointly to learning aspire,
> The men soon would yield unto them the field,
> And critics in silence admire. (P. 154)

By applauding Rowe as a crucial model for women, Little downplays Lady Mary's association with a "gay circle" and energetic social activity. On the other hand, she still marks Lady Mary as an important cultural figure. Her praise for Rowe's virtue at the expense of Lady Mary's raciness inscribes a silent encomium to Lady Mary. The fact that these models are Englishwomen suggests that Little prioritizes a precarious gendered subjectivity over a nationalist politic. For some purposes, gender legitimately transcends ethnicity. Even Little's choice of the Scotsman James Boswell as dedicatee, probably at Mrs. Dunlop's encouragement, suggests how carefully she trod a cultural, moral tightrope. Oblique comments about Burns reconfirm her view of him as a charmer of women.

The cluster of neoclassical poems from Delia to Alonzo, fashioned in a related mode to the *pastourelle* that warns against smiling, emotionally fraudulent seducers, is a case in point.[42] The poems unmask sexual practices openly; in a subtly feminized reworking of Burns's masculinist tropes, the Delia-Alonzo poems allude to uneasiness about Burns through exposing male manipulation of women which Delia cannily rejects.

Little's Alonzo first addresses Delia as the "empress of my heart" to whom "I'm urg'd to vent my pure untainted flame." In classical mythology, Delia is "a name for Diana / from her birthplace,

Delos."[43] Alonzo graphically confides that his "swelling sighs your kind attentions claim." Flattering her without mentioning marriage, he begs her to "hasten" to his arms, resign her "heart and hand," and render them in the eyes of all the muses a "happy pair" (pp. 184–85).

Alonzo is a smooth-talking rake. Delia uses Alonzo's reference to Adam to denounce the evanescence of Adam's and Eve's happiness on the basis of Eve's actions. Ironically she recommends that he learn from Adam "lest some fond nymph your pleasures all expel." She ends with a paean to celibacy that complements Little's attacks on marriage elsewhere in the volume:

> A single life we find replete with joys.
> The matrimonial chain I ever dread.
> A state of celibacy is my choice;
> Therefore Alonzo never can succeed. (P. 187)

Then in a second poem, "From Delia to Alonzo. Who Had Sent Her a Slighting Epistle," she beats him at his own game while flattering his wit and learning. She leaves his machinations and ribaldry to the reader's imagination. Alonzo sings more sweetly than Philomel, Delia avows, and flies on Pegasus, a horse with the same name as the one on which Burns, in Little's poem, "On a visit to Mr. Burns," took a hard tumble. Then she cleverly mediates her tribute, almost with a sense of eighteenth-century camp:

> That dire, deceitful creature man . . .
>   is fill'd with mazy wiles;
> His count'nance stor'd with fickle smiles:
> His flatt'ring speech too oft beguiles
>   Pure innocence. . . . (P. 189)

Rather pointedly invoking facts in Burns's life, Delia refers to Alonzo as "The laureate of our days," and goes on:

> 'Tis pity, sir, that such as you
> Should agriculture's paths pursue,
> Or destin'd be to hold the plough
>   On the cold plain;
> More fit that laurels deck'd the brow
>   Of such a swain. . . .

Delia plays with Alonzo, too, as he played with her, by speculating that he might turn out to be famous, that a future age might be

"Struck with the beauties of your page, / Old Scotia's chieftains may engage / Your name to raise" (p. 190).

Lastly, Delia trivializes Alonzo's "weak attempts" at a "ponderous theme." Regretting that love never rests within her—a knock at his rakishness—she stresses that she would never entertain a guest who would give her pain (a possible sexual reference?) and closes with the erotically ambiguous statement: "I wish you, sir, so much distress'd, / Soon well again" (p. 191).

Again indirectly but in tune with the times, "The Month's Love" addresses "maidens" who should "attend to my tale" and avoid "that sly archer" called love whose arrow kills contentment. The narrator then relates her experiences as a naive young female with an unnamed youth: "Who was the sole cause of my smart . . . / When absent from him I ador'd, / One minute as ages did prove; / Though plenty replenish'd my board, / I fasted and feasted on love" (p. 48). When she spies her suitor with Susan, she feels instant resentment and obliterates her fond memories with a warning: "But be not too forward, ye fair, / Nor take too much courage from me, / How many have fall'n in the snare / That got not so easily free?" (p. 49).

Most telling of all, however, is a poem entitled "On Seeing Mr. _____ Baking Cakes," the pointedly blank name in the title followed by an opening line that boasts an identifying signifier: Mr. Blank of the title turns out to bear the name Rab by which Robert Burns was known throughout Scotland: "As Rab, who ever frugal was, / Some oat-meal cakes was baking" (p. 171). This baker crumbles before a young female poet who enters his bakery: "a crazy scribbling lass, / Which set his heart a-quaking. / I fear, says he, she'll verses write, / An' to her neebors show it" (p. 171). These words intensify Burns's earlier offhand attentions toward Little and his soon-to-be-delivered postpublication critique of her poems that infuriates Frances Dunlop. By connecting verses with sexuality and cake, the baker implicitly blends Burns's talent with his personal focus on women. He affects not to care because everyone likes his wares.

Rather than have a customer simply glance down at his cakes, the baker prefers them to be physically touched and invites any female passerby to "put out her han' an' pree them" (p. 172). Polyvalent and heavily suggestive, *pree* is a Scots word that ranges in meaning from "experience" or "taste" to "partake of" or "kiss."[44] The sense of "to sample" is also relevant. The so-called cakes are eagerly received by the lasses. And although Mr. Blank runs away, he cries out that he has "cakes in plenty." Moreover, he can supplement the cakes with "Baith ale and porter, when I please, / To treat the lasses slily" (p. 172). The last stanza suggestively recalls the evolving legend of Burns as a man who periodically impregnates women:[45]

> Some ca' me wild an' roving youth;
> But sure they are mistaken:
> The maid wha gets me, of a truth,
> Her bread will ay be baken. (P. 172)

The speaker's submerged excoriation of Burns's carousing was a popularly held attitude, in part governed by Calvinist-related attitudes. Little herself was a burgher, a follower of the famed early eighteenth-century secessionist, the Reverend Ebenezer Erskine.[46] After agreeing toward midcentury that the burgess oath could in conscience be taken, they were known as the *new light* "burghers"; religion, they believed, was not a matter for the state but an individual matter.[47] Frances Dunlop highlights contemporary objections to Burns in one of her letters to him:

> A gentleman told me with a grave face the other day that you certainly were a sad wretch, that your works were immoral and infamous, that you lampooned the clergy and laughed at the ridiculous parts of religion, and he was told you were a scandalous free-liver in every sense of the word.[48]

Burns retorts cavalierly. He insists on his right to remain silent while claiming the privilege of spotlighting male exploits in his poems. Burns wants to titillate and respect prescribed female delicacy simultaneously.

The complex task Little sets herself—to be judicious yet subtly opinionated in public—curtails her options. In "Given to a Lady," for instance, her commentary about aristocratic charity intersects with hints about Burns's fornication that pinpoints her uncertainty about Scotland's republican hero. Little accentuates Burns's genius and his egalitarian politics, his depiction of nature and reactionary critics, yet seems to condemn his nonmarital relations with women.

Little's intermittent reservations about Burns culminate in some thematic parody. In the poem attached to the letter that she first sent Burns, she nuances Burns's persistent theme of the hurt and slighted male suitor, victim of "women's faithless vows." She parodies the poet. On a fluid sexual scale in Burns's poetry, the jilted and abused slide into each other.

Attuned to the sexual vulnerability of women, Little knows that a fallen woman is virtually unemployable, employment itself being difficult enough.[49] In other words, Little's discussion of Burns might be marking her apprehensions about the precarious position of women in her own class. Rather than attack "masters" outright, as Bridget Hill puts it:

Many husbands looked rather to their female domestics than to their wives for sexual satisfaction. What has been called "the eroticism of inequality" may in part explain the frequency with which masters are found seducing their dependent menials. It may explain the instant dismissal of servants found pregnant; mistresses must always have suspected that their husbands were responsible.[50]

Unable to expose sexual exploitation openly while being abundantly attuned to the plight of laboring women who "fell," Little could mention such common practices only through the guise of neoclassical or carefully distanced discourse. Nonetheless, however subtly encoded her opposition, she seems to use Burns as a target. She broaches subtextually what the kirk elders were authorized to execute in front of the congregation: a public assault on Burns for fornication.

All the female poets to date have tackled the same problem: how to raise the issue of gender discrimination without unduly flouting social prescription against females. Where Collier and Scott were relatively open about their anger and their quest for gender justice, Janet Little chooses a quieter route. Like Yearsley, she indicts discrimination through indirect discourse.

Burns's public contempt for the values of the kirk, an institution that dominated the life of the country, polarized discomfited contemporaries like Janet Little.[51] As an active member of the church-going community, however unorthodox certain of her views, Little censures the "Breughel quality in Ayrshire peasant life."[52]

Burns, besides, can claim additional freedoms closed to Janet Little. Through his speakers, he can openly versify his personal adventures, whereas social prescription bars Little from protesting inequitable gender relations; nor can she use an idiom close to her experience, as he does, to express offense at male-female relations. Instead, adopting English diction, she often uses rigid restricting forms.[53] Although he did not patronize her work in the formal sense, Burns helped to open Little's eyes to the condition of her existence. His prestige and presence gave her permission to explore cultural contradictions. Little recognized these complexities because she enjoyed little cultural mobility compared to Burns. Hence the need she feels to attack injustice less frontally.[54]

As an upholder of the kirk who privileges laboring-class values, Little seems to have tolerated a difficult relationship with her famed ploughman-compatriot, Robert Burns. She sides with him on democratic principles and the people's rights, she shares a knowledge of poverty that locates them in a similar relationship to middle- and upper-class people, but she flinches from his treatment of women.[55] But given Burns's popularity, even a fantasy of opposition to the local hero was scarcely allowed. Additionally, Little needs to sustain friendships with affluent people, her class—though not necessarily personal—antagonists to bolster her standing as an artist. She prides herself on her art and is prepared to fight for the chance to display it. To negotiate these varying vantage points, Little employs a form of dialectical reasoning by expressing difference while forging several informal alliances. She creates a counterdiscourse that allows for substantial slippage of meaning and a fluid political perspective. She sides with Burns against the aristocracy but rejects his free relations with women.

Thus, despite her Presbyterian frame of mind that took umbrage at Burns's high jinks and antikirk machinations, Janet Little guards her opinions; her praise of his genius allows her to move easily between the poles of conservatism and less conventional assertions of gender and class equality. As a laboring woman and a poet, her cultural solidarity with Burns challenges conservative values, opposed to her class interests, that she has assimilated. The reservations she expresses about Burns enable her to attack class superiors indirectly.

Little's use of multiple discourses from pastoral to polemic preserves social and political flexibility while appearing to internalize her position as a servant who is underwriting orthodox opinions. Concurrently she subverts upper-class domination through exposing diverse forms of corruption and employing conventional deference to her own advantage. But even Little's low-key scoffing has its limits. Inevitably, her poems betray traces of an elite culture's influence, for her class position denies her aesthetic freedom. As a self-styled "crazy scribbling lass" fused with Dunlop's "rustic damsel," notwithstanding her pragmatic use of passivity, Little cannot efface the textual influences of those she is obliged to placate and those she seeks to condemn.[56] But she is used to such complexity, even inured. Like Burns, she espouses unorthodox religious views; she is a dissenter or seceder in Presbyterian Scotland. As a new light burgher, liminality is part and parcel of her life. Always a maid and a woman with limited resources at her disposal for dissolving certain vantage points, she presents herself modestly in several poems to preserve the "correct," self-effacing demeanor expected of her. In the final poem in the volume, "To A Lady Who Sent the Author Some Paper With a Reading of Sillar's Poems," she represents herself as an untalented individual like the David Sillar of the title, one of Burns's working-class imitators. But rather disarmingly and perhaps with a self-effacing wit, she also confirms the fact that this poem ends a volume she wrote herself: "But, madam, the Muses are fled far away,/They deem it disgrace with a milkmaid to stay." Somewhat ironically, she proclaims that she will cease being a poet.

> And lest with such dunces as these I be number'd,
> The task I will drop, nor with verse be incumber'd;
> Tho' pen, ink and paper, are by me in store,
> O madam excuse, for I ne'er shall write more. (P. 207)

And Little's location may be even more intricate. Her second poem to Burns suggests an attraction for Burns that collides with her opposition to his sexual conduct. Put more bluntly, Little's understated challenge to Burns is freighted with unstated feelings for the poet whose attentions to women she deplores. Specifically, the tribute she writes to Burns on the day of his mishap suggests an attraction for the carousing poet that collides head on with her distaste for his moral license. Her playful characterization of Burns as a charmer of women who has woven a magic spell about her precedes a sexually laden stanza in which an eroticized discourse of dreams unconsciously erupts: "Oft have my thoughts, at midnight hour,/To him excursions made;/This bliss in dreams was premature,/And with my slumbers fled" (p. 111).

The reality of the poet's situation, the presence of Jean Armour, Burns's wife, his accident and the pain he suffers from a broken arm, forthrightly confront the milkmaid-poet, who initially appears awestruck. In letters to Burns, moreover, Frances Dunlop divulges on more than one occasion the importance Little attaches to meeting the famous poet:

> But talking of praise, I ought to tell you Jenny Little says you are very stupid, did not come and see her when you were at Mauchline. She is sure she would not grudge going five times as far to see you. Nay, had she not been lame . . . she might have seen the house you lived in and the reeky spence where you wrote the "Vision." I am almost hoping this will not find you at home, that you will be set out for Ayrshire to carry home your wife and son. Should that be the case, I flatter myself you

will not grudge to come a little further, either to see Jenny or me. You may trust to female vanity that each will appropriate a sufficient part of the compliment to herself. Indeed, you have experience how ready I am to catch at every instance of kindness or regard from one whose esteem I value so highly.[57]

It is not just Burns who has fallen and suffers pain; Janet Little has emotionally fallen. Hence her multivalenced sentiments about human fate comprising "alternate joy and wo" and perhaps more to the point, her erotic, anguished last stanza: "With beating breast I view'd the bard; / All trembling did him greet: / With sighs bewail'd his fate so hard, / Whose notes were ever sweet" (p. 112). Her boldness and delight in watching this domestic scenario of pain and intimacy, with the implication of a cathected relationship with Burns, renders her insensitive to some of Burns's personal and professional needs. Arguably, Burns did all he thought possible for Little.[58] Moreover, Dunlop's vigorous conservatism, her disapproval of Burns's behavior, might suggest some influence on Little's supposedly free choice of subject. Dunlop tells Burns about Little's observations of his stoicism:

> I greatly applaud that strength of mind which enables one to surmount bodily pain to such a manly pitch of fortitude as to chat at seeming ease and tranquility, as Jenny tells me you did, and entertain others with great kindness and good humor.[59]

Burns's toughmindedness strengthens Little's attachment to him. In her reactions to his poetry, she discerns a gap between what she thinks is the condition of her existence—that employers and patrons treat her well and respect her needs—and her real condition of existence—that she is permanently condescended to and patronized. She discovers tools to eschew a servile discourse. Through personal negotiations with Burns, she begins to see the construction of her gendered and class identity and, by extension, how she might oppose that construction through braiding social with confrontational verse. And there is a further hard edge to these illuminations that Burns might have provided.

Look at it this way: Robert Burns's maleness affords him a range of poetic subjects denied Janet Little. She cannot write on any subject she pleases. This issue of choice also affected Mary Collier—her patron M. B. tells how subjects were suggested to Collier; choice is less directly an issue with Hannah More, who reproaches Yearsley's quest for autonomy. How did Janet Little feel, we wonder, soliciting help from Burns and Boswell, relying on Dunlop for diverse favors, and then petitioning a twelve-year-old countess to clear the ground for publication? Since this triumvirate represents antinomic sets of values, Little is obliged to navigate rough ideological waters, the Scylla of arch conservatism on one side, the Charybdis of fornication (which Little deplores) and competition on the other. They might as well be M. B. or Hannah More—or even Mary Scott's husband, John Taylor. In her relation with these various figures of authority, Janet Little occupies the site of a subordinated subject. Individually, these supporters and patrons reflect the multiple positions in which she locates herself positively; collectively, they deny her rights and expropriate her freedom.

An early female cultural activist with a complex public self-representation, Little recognizes the vulnerability of her social position and takes pride in her gender. Her mandated thematics represent one dimension of a gendered class solidarity with such predecessors and contemporaries as working-class poets Mary Collier, the washerwoman-poet, and Ann Yearsley, the milkwoman-poet.[60]

She voices herself into the public arena—in some senses—as a community representative. A cottar's daughter, a laboring-class woman, a servant, a dairy supervisor, and a poet, she assumes multiple positions that overlap, coalesce, and separate. Little's social conditioning, in other words, yield understandable tensions and dual meanings. While allying herself with labor and against gender exploitation, she joins battle on both fronts, recognizing Burns as a class ally, as a male who psychosexually moves her. At another level, attuned to the economic and cultural precariousness of her life, Janet Little appears as an agent of traditional values, simultaneously dedicated to hierarchy and exclusion, complicitous in one way or another with those who socially dominate her.[61]

CHAPTER SEVEN

Conclusion

The texts of Mary Collier, Mary Scott, Ann Yearsley, and Janet Little demonstrate the complexity of staging female cultural history within a male hegemonic society. Refusing erasure, they refuted eighteenth-century notions of laboring female artists as unfit candidates for a career in belles lettres.[62] Transcending and affirming social prescription about women, these laboring-class poets both eulogized and excoriated such popular icons as Stephen Duck, Hannah More, and Robert Burns, intertexualizing their prose and poems to striking effect.

Reading this quartet of eighteenth-century women poets against the grain illumines the cultural construction of comparative ethnic identities and the politics of gender and class. Collier, Yearsley, and Little constitute an emerging tradition of working class poets committed to a new formulation of patriotism and national identity that inscribes issues of class and gender as part of that identity. Mary Scott complements and consolidates the worker-trio's innovative discourse by creating a continuum of aristocratic and middle-class English women writers and thereby extending cultural boundaries. Poetry may be their preferred genre, but in diverse ways these four writers also foreground their prosaic narrative power and an ability to challenge and even block out received narratives that threaten to occlude them.

Mary Collier was the first eighteenth-century woman poet-worker to underwrite laboring women and their rights. Using her class compatriot, Stephen Duck, as a gendered opponent, she reevaluates male-female relations in the agricultural workplace. She unsurprisingly defends women workers against the censure of a male laborer. Collier's poems would have stood little chance of being published had she been attacking members of her patron's class; such explicitness about bourgeois or aristocratic values would have

111

spelled cultural death. Given such a precarious political situation, Collier wrote on acceptable, promonarchy topics while inflecting her texts with an embedded opposition. In lauding the royal family as a domestic model for all Britons, Mary Collier assumes the role of devoted patriot who expects female workers to be treated on a par with men.

Yet in the autobiographical narrative to *The Woman's Labour*, she leaves readers to judge for themselves what might remain unspoken. That this veiled lament was written late in life speaks for itself. In the poems that follow, moreover, Collier undercuts her earlier feminocentric argument while tendering ardent antimarriage sentiments. Her ideological conflicts mark her complex cultural location.

With Mary Scott, the inscription of gendered national origins comes seriously into play among women poets by her vivid representation of female writers from the past and female scholarship in her own day. Siting herself alongside previous male eulogists of women, she transcends their selections (and questionable exclusions) of smart historical women; she revamps the lineage initiated by men to include neglected as well as eminent predecessors and contemporaries. In other words, she countermands the tradition of canonical male culture by choreographing a more comprehensive scenario.

Scott also reaccentuates the significance of female literary coteries and scholarship within a fluid intellectual continuum. Additionally, she furnishes a riveting new argument about the politics of identity, based preponderantly on middle-class and aristocratic texts. In so doing—her inclusion of a slavewoman and a working-class Irishwoman aside—she refocuses the definition of English, middle-class, Protestant culture.

In a laboring-class context, Ann Yearsley echoes Mary Scott in calling for an end to war and bigotry, although Scott pinpoints religious prejudice where Yearsley scorns class bias. Conflicted ideologically, like Mary Collier she extends effusive courtesies to George III, perhaps a marker of class insecurity. Functioning at a global level, Yearsley assails injustice on a wide front, from patrons and publishers like Hannah More, Thomas Cadell, and the mayor of Bristol to proslavery entrepreneurs and political tyrants across the ages.

At the start of the French Revolution, Yearsley spontaneously sides with insurgents but shifts her vantage point after the royal guillotining. Given her insecure public image, she may have deemed that level of antipatriotism too extreme. In her last volume, *Rural Lyre*, she reconfirms her patriotic support for those who originally brought glory to the British nation, commending the navy as vanguard warriors against France.

Why Mary Scott and Ann Yearsley would introduce a nationalist dimension from late midcentury to the French Revolution is scarcely surprising. Such a focus was symptomatic of the times. In Linda Colley's words:

> The Nine Years War with France, the War of Spanish Succession, and the wars against Revolutionary and Napoleonic France, all brought enough military and naval victories in their train to flatter British pride, and in most of these conflicts the victories were not only massive but durable in terms of empire won and trade routes gained. Only the War of American Independence was emphatically a defeat, and in the minds of contemporaries it was scarcely coincidental that this was also the only major war of the period in which the initial enemy confronting the British was Protestant rather than Catholic.[63]

Unlike Mary Collier and Mary Scott, however, Ann Yearsley does not specifically address the issue of women as subordinated subjects. Nonetheless, her tough-minded fight to assert her independence and her art constitutes her as a "feminist in action." Her gendered contribution derives from exemplary self-determination.

The politics of gender and class subtly inflect Janet Little's poems. On the domestic front, Little sides with class compatriot Robert Burns; on the other hand, she uses his exploits to point up discrimination against women. Moreover, in contrast to Collier, Scott, and Yearsley, Little tenders no loyalty to England and English monarchs, but is loyal exclusively—as her poem about William Wallace indicates—to Scotland. Thus Little is separate from the English poets on the question of national self-determination. She may be a class and gendered subject who sometimes allies with Collier, Scott, and Yearsley, but their ideologically distinct relationships to English national identity always divide them.

This volume, then, documents the emergence of women writers in seemingly discrete arenas of eighteenth-century poetry. On the one hand, Mary Scott belongs to the tradition of praising women inaugurated by male prose writers and poets; on the other hand, socially marginalized worker-poets establish a class-based cultural tradition while steadfastly surviving. Their texts invite a reconceptualization of tradition and patriotism as they scuttle the familiar (mythological) category of a stable white middle-class male canon. Whether lost or undervalued, all of their texts exist, in Cheryl Wall's phrase, in "intertextual relation" with one another's texts, and, more broadly, with the canon itself.[64] Transhistorically, their texts model how they collectively resisted efforts to foreclose their creativity. Instead, they redefined nation and culture in class and gendered terms, setting new rules for the cultural continuum and inviting fundamental reassessments.

NOTES

CHAPTER ONE

1. *First Feminists,* ed. Moira Ferguson (Bloomington: Indiana University Press, 1985), pp. 1–3.

2. Gerald Newman, *The Rise of English Nationalism. A Cultural History* (New York: St. Martin's Press), 1987, p. 67.

3. Benedict Anderson, *Imagined Communities: Reflections on the Origin and Spread of Nationalism* (London: Verso, 1983), p. 6.

4. Linda Colley, *Britons: Forging the Nation* (New Haven: Yale University Press, 1992), p. 46.

5. John Brewer, *The Sinews of Power. War, Money and the English State* (London: Unwin Hyman, 1989), pp. 165, 172, and passim.

6. Porter, *English Society,* p. 40. There is much debate about the role of marriage and how it affected women. See Lawrence Stone, *The Family, Sex and Marriage in England 1500–1800* (New York: Harper and Row, 1977) for an encyclopaedic account of these institutions that tends to gloss over the lives of laboring women and men. See also the following responses to Stone's work for other perspectives on the issue: Joseph Kett, "Review of the Family, Sex and Marriage," *Chronicle of Higher Education,* February 6, 1978; Christopher Hill, "Sex, Marriage and the Family in England," *Economic History Review* 31 (1978):4; Alan Macfarland, "Lawrence Stone: The Family, Sex and Marriage in England," book review, *History & Theory* 17, 1, (1979):103–25; Joan Thirsk, "The Family," *Past & Present* 27 (1964); J. H. Plumb, "Review of 'The Family, Sex and Marriage,'" *New York Review of Books,* November 24, 1977; Keith Thomas, "Review of 'Lawrence Stone, The Family, Sex and Marriage,'" *Times Literary Supplement,* October 21, 1977; E. P. Thompson, "Happy Families," *New Society* 8 (September 1977).

7. *First Feminists,* p. 24.

8. Linda Colley traces the origin of this idea: Linda Colley, *Britons,* pp. 30–33.

9. Colley, *Britons*, pp. 41, 13, and 116.

10. Colley, *Britons*, p. 35.

11. Eric Hobsbawm, "Introduction: Inventing Traditions," in *The Invention of Tradition*, ed. Eric Hobsbawm and Terence Ranger (Cambridge: Cambridge University Press, 1983), pp. 1–14. See also Peter Scott, *Knowledge and Nation* (Edinburgh: John Traves, 1990), p. 168. In 1763, the first volume of Catharine Macaulay's *History of England* appeared in which she argues—here and in the subsequent seven volumes and elsewhere in her works—that Anglo-Saxon England had been an era of popular liberties. The Norman invasion had dissolved these freedoms and since then English people had fought for their return. See particularly, Bridget Hill, *The Republican Virago: The Life and Times of Catharine Macaulay, Historian* (Oxford: Clarendon Press, 1992), p. 31ff.

12. Anderson, *Imagined Communities*, p. 6.

13. Newman, *The Rise of English Nationalism* p. 227.

CHAPTER TWO

1. Mary Collier's *The Woman's Labour* was first published (in octavo) in 1739. A second edition (also in octavo) was published in the same year. The third edition (octavo, 1740) contains a statement, dated 21 September 1739 and signed by nine Petersfield residents testifying to the "authenticity" of Mary Collier. The British Library holds a copy of this third edition. Mary Collier's title page reads as follows: "*The Woman's Labour: An Epistle to Mr. Stephen Duck; In Answer to his late Poem, called The Thresher's Labour, to which are added, The Three Wise Sentences, Taken From The First book of Esdras, Ch. III. and IV.* By Mary Collier, Now a Washerwoman, at Petersfield in Hampshire. London, Printed for the Author; and sold by J. Roberts, in Warwick-Lane; and at the Pamphlet-Shops near the Royal Exchange. 1739."

2. The British Library contains two further editions of poems by Mary Collier. One of them (with additions), entitled *Poems on Several Occasions*, 1762 (shelfmark 11632 f 12), is prefaced by "Some Remarks of the Author's Life drawn by herself." The second (shelfmark 11658 de 53) is entitled *The Poems of Mary Collier, The Washerwoman of Petersfield; To which is prefixed her Life. Drawn by Herself.* "A New Edition," Petersfield: W. Minchin. n.d. This edition contains "The Advertisement to the first edition," without the initials M. B. and with an added paragraph containing the authenticating statement of the third edition in 1740. The sizable subscribers' list to the 1762 edition of Collier's poems suggests that her employers were well known, since the names include several local titled and professional persons. Interestingly, the affluent Joliffe family members to whom Petersfield

"passed by purchase" in 1739 were not subscribers. See B. B. Woodward, Theodore C. Wilks, and Charles Lockhart, A General History of Hampshire, or The County of Southampton, Including the Isle of Wight 3 vols. (London: Virtue and Co., n.d.), 3:320.

3. See The Poems and Prose of Mary, Lady Chudleigh, ed. Margaret J. M. Ezell (Oxford: Oxford University Press, 1993); Ruth Perry, The Life and Times of Mary Astell: An Early English Feminist, Women in Culture and Society Series, ed Catharine R. Stimpson. (Chicago: University of Chicago Press, 1986); "The Veil of Chastity: Mary Astell's Feminism," Studies in Eighteenth Century Culture 9 (1979): 25–63. See also First Feminists: British Women Writers 1578–1799, ed. Moira Ferguson (Bloomington: Indiana University Press and New York: The Feminist Press, 1985), especially pp. 13–17; Hilda L. Smith, Reason's Disciples: Seventeenth-Century English Feminists (Urbana: University of Illinois Press, 1982).

4. See Elizabeth Hampsten, "Petticoat Authors: 1660–1720," Women's Studies 5, 1/2 (1980): 21–38; First Feminists, pp. 18–19.

5. Women, the Family and Freedom, ed. Susan Groag Bell and Karen M. Offen, vol. 1, 1750–1880 (Stanford, CA: Stanford University Press, 1983), especially pp. 24–27.

6. Lady Mary Wortley Montagu, The Nonsense of Common-Sense, No. 6. In Essays and Poems and Simplicity, A Comedy, ed. Robert Halsband and Isobel Grundy (Oxford: Clarendon Press, 1977).

7. Sophia's identity is still a mystery, except for the fact that her tracts are rearranged semi-translations, with substantial additions of her own of writings of a seventeenth-century French cleric, François Poulain de la Barre. Woman not Inferior to Man: or, a short and modest vindication of the natural right of the fair sex to a perfect quality of power, dignity and esteem with the Men (London: John Hawkins, 1739). Reprinted in Beauty's Triumph [London: J. Robinson, 1751]. Women's Superior Excellence over Man: or, a reply to the author of a late treatise, entitled, Man Superior to Woman. In which, the excessive weakness of that gentleman's answer to woman not inferior to man is exposed; with a plain demonstration of woman's natural right even to superiority over the men in head and heart; proving their minds as much more beautiful than the men's as their bodies are, and that, had they the same advantages of education, they would excel them as much in sense as they do in virtue. The whole interspersed with a variety of mannish characters, which some of the most noted heroes of the present age had the goodness to fight for. London. 1740 (Reprinted in Beauty's Triumph [London: J. Robinson, 1751]. François Poulain de la Barre, De l'Egalité des deux Sexes, discours physique et moral ou l'on voit l'importance de se défaire des préjugéz. Paris, 1673. In 1677 an English translation of de la Barre appeared, translated by "A. L." The Woman As Good as the Man, or, The Equality of Both Sexes (London, 1677). See also

Michael Seidel, "Poulain de la Barre's *The Woman as Good as the Man,*" *Journal of the History of Ideas* 35, 3 (1974): 499–508; C. A. Moore, "The First of the Militants in English Literature," *The Nation* 102, no. 2642 (1926): 194–96; Moira Ferguson, *First Feminists,* pp. 266–67.

8. Anon., *The Gentleman's Magazine* 9 (Oct., 1739): 525–26.

9. Walpole used the Licensing Act of 1737 to help suppress dissent "and to permit him to exercise dictatorial authority without regard for the constitutional limitations of his office." Vincent J. Liesenfeld, *The Licensing Act of 1737* (Madison: The University of Wisconsin Press, 1984), p. xi.

10. Confusion exists over Stephen Duck's early editions because his work was pirated almost immediately after he read his poems at court. An unauthorized edition, *Poems on Several Subjects,* appeared in 1730 and went into seven editions within months of the royal reading. The eighth and ninth pirated editions (like the others, in octavo) appeared in 1731 and 1733, respectively. In the preface to an allegorical poem published in 1734, *Truth and Falsehood,* Duck informs the reader that "this is the first Contract I ever made with a Printer, and consequently the *Thresher's Labour,* the *Shunamite,* etc. were never publish'd with my Approbation."

11. Autobiographical preface to expanded 1762 edition of The Woman's Labour, entitled "Some Remarks of the Author's Life drawn by herself." 2nd ed. pp. iii–iv. Note that the "New Edition" of *The Poems of Mary Collier* spells and punctuates "Some Remarks" differently. Thresher, for example, is thrasher in *A New Edition.*

12. Several social, cultural, and economic studies discuss the phenomenon of enclosure and its effect on the life of the rural labor force. Among the most useful are Roy Porter, *English Society in the Eighteenth Century,* in *The Pelican Social History of Britian* (London: Penguin Books, 1982); T. S. Ashton, *An Economic History of England: The 18th Centuury* (London: Methuen and Co., 1955); Christopher Hill (who quarrels with the view that enclosures happened peacefully, without undue detriment to country people), *Reformation to Industrial Revolution. The Pelican Economic History of Britain* (London: Penguin Books, 1968); and Raymond Williams, *The Country and the City* (New York: Oxford University Press, 1973). For the formal entry of Britain as a major power in 1713, following the Treaty of Utrecht, see John Brewer, *The Sinews of Power: War, Money, and the English State* (London: Unwin Hyman, 1989).

13. Porter, *English Society,* pp. 110, 72.

14. Porter, *English Society,* p. 226.

15. Lawrence Stone, "The Rise of the Nuclear Family in Early Modern England: The Patriarchal Stage," in *The Family in History,* ed. Charles E. Rosenberg (Philadelphia: University of Pennsylvania Press, 1975), p. 32. For

further information on the state of rural English society, see Joan Thirsk, *Agricultural Regions and Agrarian History in England. 1550–1750* (London: Macmillan Education, 1987), pp. 23–36.

16. "Between the years 1731 and 1741, nearly £50,000 was spent by Walpole on writers and printers out of the Secret Service money. . . . Walpole had found that more writers were necessary, for his long-continued absolute rule had begun to create opposition." A. S. Collins, *Authorship in the Days of Johnson: Being a Study of the Relation between Author, Patron, Publisher, and Public. 1726–1780* (London: Robert Holden, 1927), pp. 164–65. Robert Southey, *The Lives and Works of the Uneducated Poets*, ed. J. S. Childers (London: Humphrey Milford, 1925). See also *Britain in the Age of Walpole*, ed. Jeremy Black (New York: Macmillan, 1984), pp. 189–212.

17. Mary Collier, "The Woman's Labour," in *The Thresher's Labour and The Woman's Labour*, intro. Moira Ferguson (Los Angeles: University of California Press, 1985; The Augustan Reprint Society, no. 230), p. 5. All references, unless otherwise noted, will be to this edition.

18. See Louise A. Tilly and Joan W. Scott, *Women, Work, and Family* (New York: Holt, Rinehart and Winston, 1978), pp. 12–15. "Introduction," *The Woman's Labour*, pp. vi–x. For a general sense of resistance by working women to their lot, see James D. Young, *Women and Popular Struggles: A History of British Working-class Women, 1560–1984* (Edinburgh: Mainstream, 1985.

19. See Michael Roberts, "'Words They Are Women, and Deed They Are Men': Images of Work and Gender in Early Modern England," *Women and Work in Pre-Industrial England*, ed. Lindsey Charles and Lorna Duffin (London: Croom Helm, 1985), p. 154.

20. For the condition of eighteenth-century women, see Bridget Hill, *Eighteenth-Century Women: An Anthology* (London: Allen and Unwin, 1984), pp. 123–34, 156–72; and Chris Middleton, "Women's Labour and the Transition to Pre-Industrial Capitalism," in *Women and Work in Pre-Industrial England*, pp. 181–206.

21. Raymond Williams's comment about Duck is just as applicable to Mary Collier. In *The Country and the City* Williams discusses the cost to Duck of public acceptance: "It is easy to feel the strain of this labourer's voice as it adapts, slowly, to the available models in verse: the formal explanation, the anxious classical reference, the arranged subordinate clauses of that self-possessed literary manner" (p. 88).

22. *The Thresher's Labour, and The Woman's Labour*, p. 17. See also Donna Landry, "The Resignation of Mary Collier: Some Problems in Feminist Literary History," *The New Eighteenth Century: Theory, Politics English Literature* ed. Felicity Nussbaum and Laura Brown (New York and London: Methuen, 1987), p. 115.

23. For a study of Mary Collier in the context of other eighteenth-century laboring-class poets, see Donna Landry, *The Muses of Resistance: Laboring-Class Women's Poetry in Britain, 1739–1796* (Cambridge: Cambridge University Press, 1990).

24. Ivy Pinchbeck, *Women Workers and the Industrial Revolution, 1750–1850* (New York: F. S. Crofts, 1930), p. 55 and passim.

25. Dorothy M. George, *London Life in the Eighteenth Century* (New York: Capricorn, 1965), pp. x, 207–208 and passim.

26. In a letter to Moira Ferguson from Sir Alan Lubbock, he states of Collier's poem that "it gives a very interesting and credible account of life below-stairs in a big xviii century house," p. 2.

27. Advertisement, *The Woman's Labour*, pp. A2–A3.

28. Collier, *Poems on Several Occasions*, "Wise Sentences," p. 21. For information on relevant Scriptures pertaining to this, see The Anchor Bible. I and II Esdras., introd., trans., and commentary Jacob M. Myers (New York: Doubleday, 1974). I thank Robert Haller for sources and for very helpful discussions about this poem. See also Robert Young, *Analytical Concordance to the Bible on an Entirely New Plan Containing About 311,000 References, Subdivided Under the Hebrew and Greek Originals, with the Literal Meaning and Pronunciation of Each. Designed for the Simplest Reader of the English Bible. Also Index Lexicons to the Old and New Testaments, being a Guide to Parallel Passages and a Complete List of Scripture Proper Names, showing their Modern Pronunciation*. 22nd American ed., Revised Throughout by Wm. B. Stevenson, B.D. (Edin.). (New York: Funk and Wagnalls Company, 1919), pp. 1088, 1090.

29. *The Poems of Mary Collier*. A New Edition, p. vi..

30. For the wide middle-class and aristocratic encouragement of Duck compared to that extended to Collier within a limited circle of her employers, see Stephen Duck, *The Thresher's Labour*, p. iv.

31. A search of Petersfield records has so far yielded the identity of two of the signatories, Swannack and Eades: *The History of Churcher's College, Petersfield Hants, with a Sketch of the Life of Mr. Richard Churcher, The Founder; and Observations on its Management: together with a Report of the Case now pending in the High Court of Chancery, Between the Trustees and Several of the Inhabitants of Petersfield* (London: Joseph Butterworth and Son, Fleet Street, Wm Minchin, Petersfield; and all other booksellers, 1823.

32. Gerald Newman, *The Rise of English Nationalism: A Cultural History, 1740–1830* (New York: St. Martin's Press, 1987), p. 29.

33. This is the first volume mentioned in note 2.

34. *The Poems of Mary Collier . . . A New Edition* (1762) tender evidence of Mary Collier's age and her date of birth as either 1689 or 1690: in

"On the Marriage of George III" she mentioned that she wrote it in her seventy-second year. She also stated in the 1762 preface that she laundered till she was sixty-three (which would have been about 1752) and that she left Petersfield for Alton when she was seventy years old—probably in 1759. Mary Collier's age, background, and identity have been difficult to determine beyond the evidence of her texts and some circumstantial material. The West Sussex Record office shows a baptism for a Mary Collier at Heyshott, Sussex, in 1679, copied from the Bishops' Transcripts of the registers for the parish. (The original registers have not survived). The parents are Robert and Mary Collier (Collyer). There are also documents in the Cobden Archives about a Robert Collyer of Heyshott, Yeoman, which include a postnuptial settlement in 1678 by Robert and Mary Collier.

35. For the situation of married women, see Lawrence Stone, *The Family, Sex, and Marriage in England 1500–1800* (London: Weidenfeld and Nicolson, 1977). Keith Wrightson, *English Society 1580–1680* (London: Hutchinson, 1982), pp. 67–68. For insights on single women, see Rae Blanchard, "Richard Steele and the Status of Women," *North Carolina Press Studies in Philology* (404, No. 5) #3, pp. 325–55.

36. See Jean E. Hunter, "The 18th-Century Englishwoman: According to the Gentleman's Magazine," especially p. 81.

37. See Pinchbeck, *Women Workers*, pp. 53–66 and passim.

38. Colley, *Britons*, p. 32.

39. Although Christopher Smart's poem on Hannah was published later, he also used Hannah to make statements about himself. In Smart's case, Hannah represents Smart as a poet who did his great work last. In any event, the idea that Hannah "produced," despite the odds, seems to be popular among contemporaries. See *Hannah. An Oratorio*, and commentary, *The Poetical Works of Christopher Smart*, ed. Marcus Walsh and Karina Williamson, vol. 2, *Religious Poetry, 1763–1771* (Oxford: Clarendon Press, 1983), pp. 156–79.

40. Rose Mary Davis, *Stephen Duck, The Thresher-Poet* in *University of Maine Studies*, Second Series, Number 8 (Orono, Maine: University Press, 1926).

41. "Elegy upon Stephen Duck, " in *The Poems of Mary Collier. The Washerwoman of Petersfield: To Which is prefixed her Life, Drawn by Herself. A New Edition*. (Petersfield: W. Minchin, n.d.), p. 46.

42. Newman, *The Rise of English Nationalism*, pp. 67–68. For the rise of nationalism, patriotic fervor, and altercations with France, see also Linda Colley, *Britons: Forging the Nation* (New Haven: Yale University Press, 1992).

43. The body of work on nationalism that is already large includes some of the following: Benedict Anderson, *Imagined Communities: Reflec-*

tions on the Origin and Spread of Nationalism (London: Verso, 1983); Ernest Gellner, *Nations and Nationalism* (Oxford: Basil Blackwell, 1983); Elie Kedourie, *Nationalism* (London: Hutchinson, 1960); Eric Hobsbawm, *Nations and Nationalism since 1780* (New York: Cambridge University Press, 1990); Partha Chatterjee, *Nationalist Thought and the Colonial World* (Delhi: Oxford University Press, 1986).

44. Collier, "Wise Sentences," p. 44.

45. *The Anchor Bible*, commentary Jacob M. Myers, p. 55.

46. Benedict Anderson, *Imagined Communities*. See also Eve Kosofsky Sedgwick, "The Age of Wilde," in *Nationalisms and Sexualities*, ed. Andrew Parker, Mary Russo, Doris Sommer, and Patricia Yaeger (New York: Routledge, 1992), p. 236.

47. For relationship between nations and narrative, see Homi K. Bhabha, *Nation and Narration* (New York: Routledge, 1991).

48. On Zorobabel's name, see Iris V. Cully and Kendig Brubaker Cully, *From Aaron to Zerubbabel: Profiles of Bible People* (New York: Hawthorn Books, Inc. 1976); see also Robert Young, *Analytical Concordance*, pp. 1088, 1090..

49. George Trevelyan, *History of England* vol. 3 (Garden City: Doubleday and Company, Inc., 1926), p. 60.

CHAPTER THREE

1. George Rudé, *Wilkes and Liberty* (London: Lawrence and Wishart, 1962); Linda Colley, *Britons: Forging the Nation* (New Haven: Yale University Press, 1992).

2. Gerald Newman, *The Rise of English Nationalism: A Cultural History, 1740–1830* (New York: St. Martin's Press, 1987), p. 59.

3. John Duncombe, *The Feminiad; A Poem* (1754; repr. Los Angeles, 1981, The Augustan Reprint Society, no. 207). Note the confusion in spellings for the name of Duncombe's poem. Mary Scott spells it differently in her title.

4. Mary Scott, *The Female Advocate; A Poem. Occasioned by Reading Mr. Duncombe's Feminead* (1774, rpt. with intro. by Gae Holladay, Los Angeles, 1984, The Augustan Reprint Society, no. 224), p. xii. All references will be to this edition.

5. For biographical information, see *A Dictionary of British and American Women Writers 1600–1800*, ed. Janet Todd (New Jersey: Rowman and Allenheld, 1985), pp. 140–141. For the paucity of laboring writers, see

Robert Southey, *The Lives and Works of the Uneducated Poets* (London: Humphrey Milford, 1925).

6. Scott, *The Female Advocate*, p. 15.

7. For information about "female worthies" see Celeste Turner Wright, "The Elizabethan Female Worthies," in *Studies in Philology*, 43 (1946): 628–643; Natalie Zemon Davis, "'Women's History' in Transition: The European Case," *Feminist Studies*, 3 (1975–1976): 83–103; and N. Z. Davis, "Gender and Genre: Women as Historical Writers, 1400–1820," in *Beyond Their Sex: Learned Women in the European Past*, ed. Patricia H. Labalme (New York, 1980).

8. Bathsua Pell Makin, "An Essay to Revive the Antient Education of Gentlewomen: Dedication," in *First Feminists. British Women Writers 1578–1799*, ed. Moira Ferguson (Bloomington: Indiana University Press, New York: The Feminist Press, 1985), p. 13. Quoted in Myra Reynolds, *The Learned Lady in England, 1650–1760* (Boston: Houghton Mifflin, 1920), p. 27.

9. Mary Scott's publications are a complex matter seemingly tied to major events in her life. According to her correspondence with Anna Seward, John Taylor, after joining the Quakers, disapproved of "elegant arts" as worldly. Mary Scott remained a Unitarian. Seward pleaded with her to continue writing: "I am sorry to hear you confess a growing insensibility to the first and loveliest of the sciences, to which the bias of your genius originally inclined. I deplore the vexations and misfortunes which have palled and sickened those fine perceptions, whose delights might frequently soften and assuage their harrassings" (Letter 46, *Letters of Anna Seward Written Between the Years 1784 and 1807*, vol. 3 [Edinburgh: Printed by George Ramsay and Company for Archibald Constable, et al. 1811], p. 150. For further details about Mary Scott's friends, religion, and upbringing, see Moira Ferguson, "'The Cause of My Sex'": Mary Scott and the Female Literary Tradition," *Huntington Library Quarterly* 50, 4 (Autumn 1987), p vii, pp. 359–377.

10. Myra Reynolds, *The Learned Lady in England, 1650–1760* (Boston, 1920). See also George Ballard, *Memoirs of Several Ladies of Great Britain, who have been celebrated for their writings and skill in learned languages, arts and sciences* (Oxford, 1752; rpt. ed. and with intro. by Ruth Perry, New York, 1984).

11. Duncombe, *The Feminiad*, p. 15.

12. See *Letters of Anna Seward*, 2: 119. Note also the statement that Mr. Scott was a linen   merchant in "The Father of the Founder of the *Manchester Guardian*," *The Journal of the Friends Historical Society*, ed. Norman Penney. 18 (1921): 82. Since Anna Seward's father was an Anglican canon and her statement about Mr. Scott is unequivocal, it seems odd that Anna Seward was apparently incorrect; she had not, however, known Mary Scott intimately for any length of time.

According to Derek Shorrocks, there are a "few eighteenth-century Jurors books and these included an entry from Robert Scott of Milborne Port in 1752 and 1756, the first describing him as a linen weaver, the second as a yeoman (Q/RJb)." There are other references to the Scotts as linen weavers in deeds and land-tax assessments for 1747, 1766–1767, and 1794–1819.

S. G. McKay, author of *Milborne Port in Somerset*, has further informed this writer that the "table tomb of the [Scott] family" bears the name of Mary Scott's father as "John Scott, Gent." He died June 29, 1774, and is described as the son of Robert Scott, also "Gent," born in 1688, who died aged ninety in 1778. "Neither of these," McKay continues, "is described as 'Revd' or 'Priest.' . . . The case for Mary Scott's father being connected with the weaving of linen is much stronger. In the first place Milborne Port was, in the 18th century, a centre for that industry and, much to the point, a Robert Scott (whom I take to be Mary's grandfather) is mentioned in a will of William Raymond (dated 1744) and is there described as 'Linnenweaver.' . . . A surviving 'Poor Book' shows a John Scott and a Robert Scott serving consecutively as one of the two Overseers of the Poor. They also appear in the list of those who paid the poor rate." Clearly the Scotts were a well-known, somewhat distinguished Milborne Port family.

13. "Mrs. Scott, of Milborn Port; whose life was exemplary; and her loss severely felt by the poor, and lamented by her friends," *The Gentleman's Magazine* (Nov. 1787): 1024.

14. "Father of the Founder," p. 82.

15. I would like to thank Hugh F. Steele-Smith of Ilkley, West Yorkshire, most particularly for information about Mary and Anne Steele and Mary Scott. I thank him also for his transcription of this early poem by Mary Scott, stanza 2 of which is quoted in the text.

16. Much of the available information about Mary Scott and John Taylor comes in correspondence between Mary Scott and Anna Seward. See *Letters of Anna Seward*, 1: 118, 133. In a letter from Lichfield to "Miss Scott," dated 29 March 1786, Anna Seward writes:

Can it be that three months of this dreary season have elapsed, without affording me an opportunity of expressing the satisfaction I feel from perceiving you likely to renounce that painful combat with long-established affection? Ah! If the delay of Mr. Taylor's wishes were to terminate only with your mother's existence, who shall say when it may end? His lot is harder than that of Jacob toiling for his Rachael, if Hope has no distincter goal. Meantime life wears and wastes.

17. Lichfield, 20 October 1786, *Letters of Anna Seward*, 1: 187.

18. It is also possible that Anna Seward might have introduced them. The shift in Mary Scott's religious principles toward a more marked Christian persuasion is attested to in a small manuscript by Anne Steele in which

are included twenty-seven handwritten hymns by Mary Scott that accord full Trinitarian status to Jesus and the Holy Ghost. Some of the lines from several hymns are as follows:

Jesus to thy kind arms I flee
And thy attoning blood; . . .
See, at his right, the Saviour stands
And pleads attoning blood; . . .
From the same source of boundless love
His spirit he imparts.

Since the lines represent a fairly orthodox Calvinism, the hymns confirm that Mary Scott subscribed to Unitarian principles later in life.

19. Hester Mulso Chapone, *The Posthumous Works of Mrs. Chapone containing her correspondence with Mr. Richardson* 2 vols. (London: John Murray, 1807). Mary Scott and John Taylor courted for fourteen years because Scott "would not marry during the life of her aged mother." Review in *The Analytical Review*, ed. Joseph Johnson and Thomas Christie, vol. 1 (London, 1788), p. 460.

20. Again I would like to thank Hugh F. Steele-Smith for this information about Mary and Anne Steele and Mary Scott.

21. Florence E. Skillington, *The Coltmans of the Newarke at Leicester* in *Transactions of the Leicestershire Archaelogical Society* (Leicester: W. Thornley and Son, 1934–1935), p. 23.

22. In addition to Scott's own literary group, it seems clear that numerous female literary groups had existed for almost a century. The community around Astell is described in Ruth Perry's biography of Mary Astell, *The Celebrated Mary Astell: An Early English Feminist* (Chicago, University of Chicago Press, 1986). The seventeenth-century writer Jane Barker is said by William H. McBurney to have "continued the tradition" of Katherine Philips's group or "Society of Friendship." See McBurney, "Edmund Curll, Mrs. Jane Barker, and the English Novel," *Philological Quarterly* 37 (1958): 385–399. The Thynne set at Longleat, Somerset, receives attention in Helen Sard Hughes, *The Gentle Hertford: Her Life and Letters* (New York, Macmillan, 1940) and in Henry F. Stecher, *Elizabeth Singer Rowe: The Poetess of Frome: A Study of Eighteenth-Century English Pietism* (European University Papers, Series 14, *Anglo-Saxon Language and Literature*, vol. 5: Bern: Herbert Lang, 1973). Joanna Lipking deduces that the feminist polemicist Eugenia may have been tied to the Longleat circle because of the dedication to Lady Worseley.

23. *Bluestocking Letters*, ed. R. Brimley Johnson (London: John Lane, 1926), p. 147.

24. M. G. Jones, *Hannah More* (Cambridge: Cambridge University Press, 1952), p. 47.

25. See Sylvia Myers, *The Bluestocking Circle: Women, Friendship, and the Life of the Mind in Eighteenth-Century England* (Oxford: Clarendon Press, 1990), pp. 124–26.

26. Myers, *The Bluestocking Circle*, pp. 124–125. See Anon, *The Gentleman's Magazine* 9 (1739): 525–26.

27. *A Description of Millenium Hall and the Country Adjacent: together with the Characters of the Inhabitants, and such historical anecdotes and Reflections, as may excite in the reader Proper Sentiments of Humanity, and lead the Mind to the Love of Virtue. By a Gentleman on his Travels* (London: for T. Carnan, 1762. Reprint. Ed. and intro. by Walter M. Crittenden. New York: Bookman Associates, 1955).

28. Female circles also emulated the Bluestockings in the provinces. Lady Miller's Batheaston assembly, which Fanny Burney, Sarah Fielding, and Anna Seward visited, is discussed in detail in Ruth Avaline Hesselgrave, *Lady Miller and the Batheaston Literary Circle* (New Haven: Yale University Press, 1927).

29. In 1803, with the appearance of *Memoirs of Illustrious Women* by Mary Hays—also a feminist polemicist in her own right—one of the first nineteenth-century "encyclopaedies" of "female worthies" and a new chapter in feminist literary history were inaugurated. Robert Southey added a few women's names to *Specimens of the Later English Poets*, and thirty women are mentioned briefly in Alexander Chalmer's *General Biographical Dictionary*, but only at midcentury did books appear that were solely devoted to women—Louisa Stuart Costello, Sarah Josepha Hale, Jane Williams, and Julia Kavanaugh were among the authors. As showpieces or literary museums for women's uncontroversial writings, their entries virtually exclude protest writings; even Hays's *Memoirs* principally derives from Ballard's text. Adulation rather than critical assessment characterizes the approach of their works. Ironically, neither Scott's nor Wollstonecraft's name merits a mention.

In Matilda Bentham's *Biographical Dictionary of the Celebrated Women of Every Age and Country* (1804), for example, only Macaulay and Robinson among contemporary radicals rank inclusion. Macaulay is described as "pleasing and delicate in her person, and a woman of great feeling and indisputable abilities, though the democratic spirit of her writings has made them fall into disrepute." Robinson is termed a "woman of great abilities" who "preferred feelings to justice in her morality" (presumably a reference to her liaison with the Prince of Wales), and possessed a muse "melancholy, tender, and harmonious." Valued above all is evidence of propriety and subdued sensibilities.

30. Letter 46, *Letters of Anna Seward Written Between the Years 1784 and 1807* vol. 3 (Edinburgh: Printed by George Ramsay and Company for Archibald Constable, et al., 1811), p. 150. Mary Scott's son, who founded the *Manchester Guardian*, appears to have followed in his mother's ideological footsteps; he appealed to people to claim their own agency.

31. Mary Poovey, *The Proper Lady and The Woman Writer: Ideology as Style in the Works of Mary Wollstonecraft, Mary Shelley, and Jane Austen* (Chicago and London: The University of Chicago Press, 1984), p. 28.

32. Janet Todd, *A Dictionary of British and American Women Writers 1600–1800* (New Jersey: Rowman & Allenheld, 1985), p. 300; George Ballard, *Memories*, pp. 393–395.

33. For a discussion of Mary Scott's inclusion of Phillis Wheatley, see Moira Ferguson, *Subject to Others: British Women Writers and Colonial Slavery, 1678–1834* (New York: Routledge, 1992), pp. 113–115, 125–129.

34. See Peter Fryer, *Staying Power: The History of Black People in Britain* (London, Pluto, 1984), pp. 133–190, and passim; Winthrop Jordan, *White Over Black: American Attitudes toward the Negro, 1550–1812* (Chapel Hill: University of North Carolina Press, 1968), pp. 257–259, 273–281, and passim; Folaris O. Shyllon, *Black Slaves in Britain* (Oxford, 1974). See also Paul Edwards and James Walvin, *Black Personalities in the Era of the Slave Trade* (Baton Rouge, 1983), pp. 42–53 and passim.

35. Barbara Brandon Schnorrenberg, "Catherine Macaulay Graham: The Rise and Fall of a Female Intellectual." (Paper read at the annual meeting of the American Society for Eighteenth-Century Studies, University of Pennsylvania, Philadelphia, 1975).

36. Thomas Seward includes these lines in "The Female Right to Literature, in a Letter to a Young Lady, from Florence." In Robert Dodsley, *Collection of Poems by Several Hands* (London, 1748), vol. 2, pp. 295–302.

37. Mary Scott was well aware of male commendatory verse and its "dramatis personnae." This awareness of male poets of earlier periods is evident in her choice of Elizabeth Cooper, for Cooper, in her extensive anthology of male poets entitled *The Muses Library*, published in 1737 and 1741, includes poems that range from the eleventh century to the Renaissance, all written by men. See Elizabeth Cooper, *The Muses Library; or, a Series of English Poetry* . . . Huntington Library Shelfmark, 261953 (London: James Hodges, 1741).

38. Note also the preface dedicated to Mary Steele and the tribute extended to her in the concluding lines. Mary Steele was a poet in her own right who for several years seems to have viewed Mary Scott as a mentor as well as a friend. Mary Steele also refers to the unknown Celia who died young, clearly a close friend of both Scott and Mary Steele.

39. *A Dictionary*, ed. Todd, p. 197. See also *The Feminist Companion to Literature in English: Women Writers from the Middle Ages to the Present.* Ed. Virginia Blain, Patricia Clements, Isobel Grundy (New York: Yale University Press, 1990), p. 648.

40. Elizabeth Tollett, *Poems on Several Occasions. With Anne Boleyn to King Henry VIII. An Epistle* (London: John Clarke, 1755).

41. *A Dictionary*, ed. Todd, p. 225; The *Feminist Companion*, ed. Blain, Clements, Grundy, pp. 760–761.

42. See Kate Hurt-Mead, *A History of Women in Medicine from the Earliest Times to the Beginning of the 19th Century* (Haddam, Conn.: The Haddam Press, 1938). Medicine had not advanced extensively in the eighteenth century: Hurd-Mead reminds us that a popular potion to assuage uterine cancer contained (among other items) lapis lazuli, whey, and black hellebore. The *cervix uteri* was then anointed with such substances as goose grease, hen's fat, lilies, wax, and oil of capers; then below the navel a paste of figs, pennyroyal, and linseed boiled in water was applied, followed by an injection into the vagina of all the above used oils "together with the marrow of veal bone, hen's grease and yolk of egg. The patient is to eat no salt meat, pork, fish, or cheese" (p. 465). Less spectacularly for Mary Scott's failing eyesight, the evangelical Methodist John Wesley would have presribed the juice of rotten apples and for her bleeding "an application of cobwebs" (p. 518).

43. In a foreboding letter of July 29, 1792, for example, in response to one from Mary Scott, Anna Seward hinted at the misfortunes that precipitated Scott's death the following year. "We have each had long and painful experience of sickness and of sorrow," confided Seward, "since the year commenced; but you are at present blest with two fine children. I trust they will live to repay you yet more and more for the increase of pain and debility which their birth and infant nurture cost you." . . . The Bristol and Somerset Register of Burials records that Mary Scott Taylor died on 5 June 1793, aged forty-one.

44. Mary Scott's final plea in her poem for "sweet retirement's shady bow'rs, / [in] studious care, to spend my remnant / hours" could well be a complicated personal wish, masquerading as desire for a socially acceptable rural retreat that had attracted the somewhat affluent middle class people and the aristocracy for well over a century, at least since John Milton had proposed the beauties of solitude in *Il Penseroso:* "And may at last my weary age / Find out the peaceful hermitage" (*The Portable Milton*, ed. Douglas Bush [New York: Viking, 1949], p. 70). Poems on that subject abounded. Before and after *The Female Advocate*, poets acclaimed rural retreat as life's desideratum, the optimum modus vivendi. Scott may also have known Sarah Dixon's volume, *Poems on Several Occasions* (1740), that included "Retirement," Sir Thomas Warton the Elder's poem, and William Cowper's poem of 1781 on that subject. The retirement of Lady Eleanor Butler and the Honorable Sarah Ponsonby and their subsequent renown testifies to the continuity of this activity in Scott's lifetime. Scott's friend, Anna Seward, had visited the Ladies of Llangollen and had written a popular poem in their honor. On the other hand, Scott may have voiced a longing for retirement because her health was deteriorating on account of popular medicine and she could not marry while her mother was very ill, required constant care, and disapproved of the match. In the poem, Scott could vent pent-up frustration and a desire to be removed from all this stress. Sarah Dixon, *Poems on*

Several Occasions (Canterbury: J. Abree, 1740); *The Three Wartons: A Choice of Their Verse*, ed. Eric Partridge (London: Scholastic Press, 1927), p. 40. See, for example, Elizabeth Mavor, *The Ladies of Llangollen: A Study in Romantic Friendship* (London: Michael Joseph, 1971), pp. 136–37 and passim; Anna Seward, *Llangollen Vale with Other Poems*, Huntington Library shelfmark 315393 (London: G. Sael, 1796), pp. 1–11.

45. For a compelling discussion of "scandalous memoirists," see Felicity Nussbaum, *The Autobiographical Subject: Gender Ideology in Eighteenth-Century England* (Baltimore and London: Johns Hopkins University Press, 1989), pp. 178–200.

46. *The Analytical Review*, vol. 1 (London, 1788), p. 460.

47. *The Critical Review: or, Annals of Literature* (London: A. Hamilton, 1774), pp. 216–220.

48. *The Gentleman's Magazine, and Historical Chronicle*, vol. 44 (London, 1774), p. 376.

49. *The Monthly Review; or, Literary Journal*, vol. 51 (London, 1774), p. 389.

50. Elizabeth Benger, *The Female Geniad: A Poem* (London, 1791). See also footnote 29.

51. *Messiah: A Poem, In Two Parts. Published for the benefit of the General Hospital at Bath.* (Bath, 1788). In *The Analytical Review* for 1788 (p. 460), the reviewer makes the following comment: "We cannot help thinking, that when Miss Scott first appeared as a writer [in a poem entitled *The Female Advocate*], her exertions were more vigorous than on the present occasion. Subjects of the religious kind are, in our estimation, not the most favourable to poetry. At least, they require talents of uncommon excellence to render them poetically interesting. This is, however, perhaps the first poem on the subject written by a Unitarian." Emanuel Green lists the poem in *Bibliotheca Somersetensis* (1902).

52. I thank Hugh F. Steele-Smith for the transcription of "Stanzas Written at Yeo."

CHAPTER FOUR

1. *Monthly Review*, Nov. 1791, p. 347; see also *Gentleman's Magazine* 54 (1784): p. 897.

2. Robert Southey, *The Lives and Works of the Uneducated Poets*, ed. J. S. Childers (London: 1925); Chauncy Brewster Tinker, *Nature's Simple Plan: A Phase of Radical Thought in the Mid-Eighteenth Century* (Princeton, 1922), 92; and Rayner Unwin, *The Rural Muse: Studies in the Peasant Poetry*

of England (London, 1954). For further biographical information about Ann Yearsley's early life, see Donna Landry, *The Muses of Resistance: Laboring-Class Women's Poetry in Britain, 1739–1796* (Cambridge: Cambridge University Press, 1990); Mary Waldron, "Ann Yearsley and the Clifton Records," *Age of Johnson* III (1990); and Moira Ferguson, "Resistance and Power in the Life and Writings of Ann Yearsley," in *Eighteenth-Century Theory and Interpretation* 27, 3 (1986), p. 247.

3. "An Historical Milkwoman," Anon, *Chamber's Journal*, n.d.; rpt. *The Eclectic Magazine*, March 1856, pp. 393–98.

4. Information and quotations in this paragraph come from J. M. S. Tompkins, "The Bristol Milkwoman," in *The Polite Marriage: Eighteenth Century Essays* (Cambridge, 1938), pp. 62–63.

5. In Mary Mahl and Helene Koon, *The Female Spectator: English Women Writers before 1800* (Bloomington, 1977), pp. 277–78.

6. Mahl and Koon, *The Female Spectator*, p. 279.

7. Mahl and Koon, *The Female Spectator*, p. 280.

8. Tompkins, "The Bristol Milkwoman," p. 60.

9. "An Historical Milkwoman," p. 394.

10. Ann Yearsley, "A Prefatory Letter to Mrs. Montagu. By Miss Hannah More." *Poems on Various Subjects* (London, 1787), pp. ix. Note that in the first volume *Poems on Several Occasions*, 1785, the authorship of the prefatory letter is not given.

11. Raymond Dexter Havens, *The Influence of Milton on English Poetry* (New York, 1961), pp. 655–56.

12. Eleanor M. Sickels, *The Gloomy Egoist: Moods and Themes of Melancholy from Gray to Keats* (New York, 1932), pp. 137–38. See also Amy Louise Reed, *The Background of Gray's Elegy: A Study in the Taste for Melancholy Poetry 1700–1751* (New York, 1924).

13. See *The Thresher's Labour* and *The Woman's Labour*, "Introduction" (Los Angeles, 1985), pp. iii-xii.

14. In Odell Shepard and Paul Spencer Woods, eds. *English Prose and Poetry 1660–1800* (New York: 1934), p. 501.

15. Ann Yearsley, *Poems on Several Occasions* (London: T. Cadell, 1785), p. 72, All other references will be to this edition.

16. Mahl and Koon, *The Female Spectator*, pp. 283–284.

17. For an account of the relationship, including the later dispute between Hannah More and Ann Yearsley, see William Roberts, *Memoirs of*

the Life and Correspondence of Mrs. Hannah More (London, 1834), pp. 361–75, 383–91; and M. G. Jones, *Hannah More* (Cambridge, 1952), pp. 73–76. Hannah More also chronicled the dispute in correspondence with Lady Middleton (Georgiana, Lady Chatterton, *Memorials . . . of Admiral Lord Gambier* [London, 1861], pp. 147–53). Another source of contemporary information, like Roberts favoring More, comes from Henry Thompson, *The Life of Hannah More* (London, 1838). Yearsley offered her account in the apparatus to the fourth edition of her first volume, *Poems on Several Occasions*, in "To the Noble and Generous Subscribers," and at least the first edition of her second volume. A. D. Harvey points out that the relationships between material property, the security of the middle class, and awareness of poverty caused the Bluestockings to be fashionably benevolent (A. D. Harvey, *English Poetry in a Changing Society, 1780–1825* [London: Allison and Busby], p. 40). F. K. Prochaska elaborates on the specific middle-class female involvement in philanthropy in *Women and Philanthropy in Nineteenth-Century England* (Oxford: Clarendon Press, 1980).

18. Ann Yearsley, *Poems on Various Subjects* (London: Printed for the Author and Sold by G. G. J. and J. Robinson, 1787), p. xx.

19. Although public focus on Yearsley's private circumstances somewhat diminished during her writing decade, 1785–1795 approximately, reviewers never failed to comment—often in condescending tones—on her profession and on the novelty of a milkwoman-writer. The more she persevered, the more they took her seriously as an independent writer. See *Monthly Review*, September 1785, pp. 216–17, and December 1787, pp. 485–89.

20. Mary Alden Hopkins, *Hannah More and Her Circle* (New York, 1947), pp. 124–125, 130; Annette Meakins, *Hannah More: A Biographical Study* (London, 1911), p. 16.

21. "Mrs. Yearsley's Narrative," *Poems on Various Subjects*, p. xxiv. In the thirty poems of volume 2, eleven center on death, affliction, and other difficult issues.

22. *Autobiography of Mrs. Fletcher* (Edinburgh, 1876), pp. 29–30.

23. *Early Recollections* (London, 1837), pp. 69–79.

24. How the family came to these dire straits is unclear. Hannah More called John Yearsley "honest and sober," and a correspondent to the *Gentleman's Magazine*, Dec. 1784, depicted him as a man "of no vice but little capacity." He and Ann Yearsley were married in 1774. He died in 1803. See also Mary Waldron, "Ann Yearsley and the Clifton Records," footnote 2.

25. *Poem on the Inhumanity of the Slave-Trade* (London, 1788), sig. B. All references will be to this edition.

26. Ann Yearsley, *Stanzas of Woe*, J. J. Robinson (London, 1790), pp. 6–7. All references will be to this edition.

27. Abraham H. Lass, David Kireidijian, and Ruth M. Goldstein, *The Facts on File. Dictionary of Classical, Biblical and Literary Allusions* (New York and Oxford: Facts on Film Publications, n.d.), p. 65.

28. I thank Elaine Hobby for presenting me with a fair copy of *The Dispute*, n.d.

29. Ann Yearsley, *Earl Goodwin* (London, 1791), p. 42.

30. Gerald Newman, *The Rise of English Nationalism: A Cultural History 1740–1830* (New York: St. Martin's Press, 1987), pp. 227–29.

31. Yearsley's choice of subject matter involving power relationships was common in the works of British radicals before and after the French Revolution. See Gary Kelly, *The English Jacobin Novel* (Oxford: Oxford University Press, 1976).

32. Lawrence Stone, "The Rise of the Nuclear Family in Early Modern England: The Patriarchal Stage," in *The Family in History*, ed. Charles E. Rosenberg (Philadelphia: University of Pennsylvania Press, 1975), p. 32.

33. Newman, *The Rise of English Nationalism*, p. 236.

34. Waldron, "Ann Yearsley and the Clifton Records," p. 315.

35. Ann Yearsley, "Reflections on the Death of Louis XVI" Bristol: Printed for and Sold by the Author, 1793; "An Elegy on Marie Antoinette of Austria, Ci-devant Queen of France": with a Poem on the Last Interview between the King of Poland and Loraski. No place or date of publication given, probably Bristol. J. Rudhall is the printer. Handwritten if the Harvard volume is Bristol, 1795; "Sequel to Reflections on the Death of Louis XVI." Bristol: Printed for and Sold by the Author, 1793.

36. "Poem on the Last Interview between the King of Poland and Loraski." The reason for Yearsley's yoking of the three poems on doomed French royalty and Loraski is unclear. Very likely, she wants to underline her distaste for enforced death, also seen in her anti-slavery poem.

37. Ann Yearsley, *The Rural Lyre; A Volume of Poems* (London: G. G. and J. Robinson, 1796). All references will be to this edition.

38. Newman, *The Rise of English Nationalism*, p. 230.

39. Newman, *The Rise of English Nationalism*, p. 116.

40. Catharine Macaulay, *The History of England from the Revolution to the Present Time in a Series of Letters to a Friend [The Revd. Dr. Wilson]*, Bath, 1778, vol. 1 p. 5, quoted in Bridget Hill, *The Republican Virago: The Life and Times of Catharine Macaulay* (Oxford: Clarendon Press, 1992), p. 31.

41. Christopher Hill argues that Catharine Macaulay's articulation of this theory in the eight volumes of *The History of England* was an "impor-

tant landmark." See Christopher Hill, *Puritanism and Revolution* (London: Penguin, 1986), p. 99; and Catharine Macaulay, *The History of England from the Accession of James I to that of the Brunswick Line.* 8 vols, London: 1763–1783, vol. 1, p. 5 and passim.

42. A. L. Morton, *A People's History of England* (New York: International Publishers, 1938), pp. 350–52.

43. In *The Industrial Muse: A Study of Nineteenth-Century Working-Class Literature* (New York: Barnes and Noble, 1974), Martha Vicinus compares the encouragement and subsequent abandonment of eighteenth-century laboring poets (almost always male) with the situation of their nineteenth-century laboring-class male poet counterparts whose patrons found it "socially necessary to foster working men who accepted middle-class superiority," palpably an acknowledgment that Yearsley rejected (pp. 168–79).

CHAPTER FIVE

1. For further information, see Moira Ferguson, "The Unpublished Poems of Ann Yearsley," in *Tulsa Studies in Women's Literature* (Spring 1993), pp. 13–46.

2. "To Stella" with its superscription appears on the first page following the printed volume. I assume that the "several Pieces" refers to "To Stella" and the poems that immediately follow in the subsequent blank pages.

3. See Hannah More's letter to Elizabeth Montagu, October 20, 1784, published as part of the prefatory apparatus to Ann Yearsley's first volume of poems. Ann Yearsley, "A Prefatory Letter to Mrs. Montagu," *Poems on Various Subjects* (London, 1787), p. x.

4. Ann Yearsley may have read a contemporary essay on that subject. Vicesimus Knox, "On the Fear of Appearing Singular," *Essays Moral and Literary. A New Edition of Two Volumes*, vol. 1, no. 5 (London: Charles Dilly, 1782), pp. 21–22. As an indication of Knox's continuing popularity, Mary Wollstonecraft later quotes from him in *A Vindication of the Rights of Woman* (1792). Note, also, Margaret Doody's smart discussion of Yearsley's deliberate adoption of classical terms in defiance of social prescription for women of her class. Margaret Doody, *The Daring Muse: Augustan Poetry Reconsidered* (Cambridge, 1985), p. 130.

5. For Hannah More's activities in these early years, and her relationship with Ann Yearsley and their dispute, see William Roberts, *Memoirs of the Life and Correspondence of Mrs. Hannah More*, vol. 1 (London, 1834), pp. 361–75 and 383–91. See also M. G. Jones, *Hannah More* (Cambridge, 1952), pp. 73–76. Hannah More also chronicled the dispute in correspon-

dence with Lady Middleton: Georgiana, Lady Chatterton, *Memorials . . . of Admiral Lord Gambier* (London, 1861), pp. 147–53. For biographical and critical information on Ann Yearsley and her texts, see Donna Landry, *The Muses of Resistance: Laboring-Class Women's Poetry in Britain, 1739–1796* (Cambridge: Cambridge University Press, 1990); Mary Waldron, "Ann Yearsley and the Clifton Records," *Age of Johnson*, 3 (1990) p. 301; and Moira Ferguson, "Resistance and Power in the Life and Writings of Ann Yearsley," in *Eighteenth-Century Theory and Interpretation*, 27, 3 (1986), p. 247. For further data about Ann Yearsley's cultural place among urban and rural laboring class poets, see Robert Southey, *The Lives and Works of the Uneducated Poets*, ed. J. S. Childers (London, 1925); Chauncy Brewster Tinker, *Nature's Simple Plan: A Phase of Radical Thought in the Mid-Eighteenth Century* (Princeton, 1922), p. 92; and Rayner Unwin, *The Rural Muse: Studies in the Peasant Poetry of England* (London, 1954).

6. Guillermo Gómez-Peña, "A Binational Performance Pilgrimage," *Third Text: 3rd World Perspectives in Contemporary Art and Culture*, vol. 19 (Summer 1992), p. 73.

7. One biographer states the situation as follows: "When one of the Lords of the Bedchamber, Fauconberg, offered his house at Cheltenham for royal recuperation, George accepted; and after Parliament's prorogation in July he proceeded there with the Queen and the Princesses Charlotte, Augusta, and Elizabeth, to take the medicinal waters and try the restorative virtues of this small but genteel resort. The water, the King persuaded himself, proved 'salutary.'" (John Brooke, *King George III* [New York: McGraw-Hill, 1972], p. 322.)

8. Queen Charlotte further affirms the king's popularity and his delight in talking to members of the general population: "The crowds of people were immense," she states, "and to give you a small idea of it at Rodbury the magistrates computed the number of people for that day only to have been between fifty and six thousand. . . . He went into people's houses, saw them at work, and asked how they lived. All this he had done at Windsor for years. The importance of the Cheltenham visit is that his doings were reported in the newspapers and the whole country learnt about them." (John Brooke, *King George III* [New York: McGraw-Hill, 1972], p. 323.)

9. Stanley Ayling, *George the Third* (New York: Alfred A. Knopf, 1972), pp. 329–32.

10. "Elegy Written on the Banks of the Avon," *Poems on Various Subjects* (London: Printed for G. G. J. and J. Robinson, 1787), p. 41. For information about Mary Smith's drowning, see "Elegy," *Poems on Various Subjects*, p. 38.

11. "On the Death of Mr Smith, Surgeon," was published in Clifton, June 29, 1791. The surgeon Richard Smith died of a relapse from fever on June 21, 1791, several years after the death of the Richard Smith mentioned

in the elegy. Whether Ann Yearsley knew the Smith family of "Elegy" is unknown, and this attribution of Horatio as the Richard Smith of the footnote is speculative. The poem is entitled "To Mr. G . . .," who also remains unknown, and the drowned three-year-old son has been transposed to a daughter in the unpublished poem. I thank Dawn Dyer for helpful information. For Richard Smith, surgeon—an acquaintance of Ann Yearsley—see G. Munro Smith, *A History of the Bristol Royal Infirmary* (Arrowsmith, 1917), pp. 460–63. The Bristol directories for 1785 list the surgeon and a Richard Smith "hardware man and buckle master" (*Bristol Directory*, 1785, p. 50). By 1793, no Richard Smiths are listed, making it at least possible that the drowned Richard Smith was the "hardware man." Note also that a handwritten note from Ann Yearsley to the surgeon Richard Smith in 1790 states that she encloses her poems and is grateful to him for his support. In terms of publication, the inscription on the letter, "Sent with the poems to Mr. R. Smith Surgeon," suggests that she was sending the second volume since only individual occasional poems were published between 1787 and 1790.

12. "The Unpublished Poems," pp. 35–37, 39–41.

13. See "Elegy," *Poems on Several Occasions*, p. 41.

14. Linda M.-G. Zerilli, in George Levine, *Constructions of the Self* (New Brunswick: Rutgers University Press, 1992), p. 198.

15. *A Dictionary of Philosophy*, ed. Antony Flew (New York: St. Martin's Press, 1979), p. 206.

16. William S. Sahakian, *History of Philosophy* (New York: Barnes and Noble Books, 1968), pp. 17–20.

17. The handwritten and printed versions of "To William Cromartie Yearsley" differ somewhat. The poem is attached to the printed version of *Stanzas of Woe*, 1790. Several lines are added to the final version. For example,

For thee, each devious Labyrinth will explore,
Thro' which the sons of Greece have gone before.
With him then safely tread the mazy round,
In ev'ry step, a grand ascent is found.

The most striking difference is in two handwritten lines that originally read, "The brave ne'er own a wretch who dares to boast / Beauty thus wreck'd on bleak affliction's coast." The original two lines talk about men fleeing from a boastful woman, even when their mistreatment is the source of her boastfulness. Substituted for the two lines are four printed lines that talk about how an uneducated or miseducated woman always seeks peace of mind in her own appearance and this causes her to hurt the man she loves. These printed lines are more reasoning and apologetic about the mistreatment and resulting faults of women.

18. "To William Cromartie Yearsley," p. 30.

19. *Rural Lyre; A Volume of Poems* (London: Printed for G. G. and J. Robinson, 1796). With its curious admixture of Roman history (four poems constitute over one-third of the volume) and elegies, together with a short but poignant verse dialogue from a shepherdess to Colin and an address to her patron, *Rural Lyre* is a distinct change of pace. Although it does talk at a displaced level about Yearsley's political concerns, it appears, at least superficially, as a much less personal text.

20. For a short and generally helpful account of repression that could result, say, in overcompensation, see *Feminism and Psychoanalysis: A Critical Dictonary*, ed. Elizabeth Wright (Oxford: Blackwell, 1992), pp. 382–84.

21. For a compelling argument about multiple subjectivities, see Gomez-Peña, "A Binational Performance Pilgrimage," pp. 65–78.

22. J. M. S. Tompkins, "The Bristol Milkwoman," *The Polite Marriage: Eighteenth-Century Essays* (Cambridge, 1938), pp. 99–101.

CHAPTER SIX

1. Janet Little, *The Poetical Works of Janet Little. The Scotch Milkmaid* (Ayr: Printed by John & Peter Wilson, 1792). All references will be to this edition. (Please note this edition is mispaginated.)

2. James Paterson, *The Contemporaries of Burns and The More Recent Poets of Ayrshire* (Edinburgh: Adam Hugh Paton, 1840).

3. *Robert Burns and Mrs. Dunlop. Correspondence Now Published in Full for the First Time*, vol. 1, ed. William Wallace, 2 vols. (New York: Dodd, Mead, and Company, 1898), p. 190. Frances Anna Wallace Dunlop was "fiercely conservative in all matters of morality" (p. xv). Connected by blood with the renowned Scottish hero William Wallace, she married John Dunlop of a distinguished Ayrshire family in 1748 and was widowed in 1785. The castle or mansion house of the Dunlops was in Cunninghame, Ayrshire. Note, too, that Janet Little's literacy was not a given at this time. See Frances Dunlop's comment to Robert Burns:

> "The polish of western manners at that time was great, so that we find the *belles-lettres* cultivated by all stations, particularly among the female sex. In Aug. 1789 a chamber-maid in Ayrshire, the early residence of the above-mentioned bard, wrote in the dialect of the country some poems, of which we have the following lines remaining. Her name was Janet Little, but critics dispute whether she had it from her father, or because her genius was believed of the dwarfish kind—a species of stature and wit then imported into Britain by the famous Count Boro-

wastic, and from thence greatly admired and sure of making the possessor's fortune or immortalizing his memory." (*Robert Burns and Mrs. Dunlop: Correspondence*, vol. 1, p. 299).

It was probably not as easy for laboring women to be as literate as men in the eighteenth century, although the myth of Scottish poverty tied to literacy has long been laid to rest. See *The Poems and Songs of Robert Burns*, ed. James Kinsley, vol. 3 (Oxford: Clarendon Press, 1968), p. 973. For details of Scottish education at the time of Burns and Little, see Alexander Law, "Scottish Schoolbooks of the Eighteenth and Nineteenth Centuries," *Studies in Scottish Literature*, ed. G. Ross Roy, vol. 28 (Columbia: University of South Carolina, 1983), pp. 1–32.

4. In 1789, Susan Dunlop had married a French refugee and landed proprietor, James Henri. For the Countess's lineage, see *The Complete Peerage of George Edward Cockayne*, revised and enlarged by Vicary Gibbs (London: St. Catherine Press, 1932), vol. 8, p. 163.

5. Robert Burns also had a connection with the Earl of Loudoun. Burns and his brother Gilbert subleased Mossgiel Farm from Gavin Hamilton—dedicatee of Burns's first volume of poems—though not directly from the earl.

6. J. D. Mackie, *A History of Scotland* (Middlesex: Penguin Books Ltd., 1964), p. 319. Since the cost of living in Ayrshire had doubled between 1740 and 1790, butter was now 9d. a pound. Janet Little's job was invaluable. See Marjorie Plant, *The Domestic Life of Scotland in the Eighteenth Century* (Edinburgh: Edinburgh University Press, 1952), p. 109.

7. For information about Ayrshire and dairy farming at this time, see John Strawhorn, *Ayrshire in the Time of Burns* (Ayr: Archaelogical Natural History Society, 1959); James Handley, *The Agricultural Revolution in Scotland* (Glasgow: Burns, 1963); William Fullerton, *General View of the Agriculture of the County of Ayr, with Observations on the Means of Its Improvement* (Edinburgh: Printed by John Paterson, 1793).

8. James Kinsley calls Burns's humble description of himself in the preface a "calculated appeal to critical orthodoxy" (*The Poems and Songs of Robert Burns*, p. 972); David Daiches notes his "deliberate public appearance"; see his *Robert Burns* (New York: Macmillan, 1966), p. 103; A. M. Kinghorn talks of Burns striking a pose; see his, "The Literary and Historical Origins of the Burns Myth," *Dalhousie Review* 39 (1959), pp. 76–85. On the other hand, James Currie quotes Dugald Steward on the range of Burns's early education, in James Kinsley "Contemporary Impressions of Robert Burns" in *The Poems and Songs*, p. 1535. For an English standardization of Burns's cultural self-portrait, see Robert Southey, *The Lives and Works of the Uneducated Poets*, ed. J. S. Childers (London: 1925). For Burns's instant popularity with the cross-class British public, see James Kinsley, *The Poems and Songs*, pp. 975–76. Not unlike Little, Burns had one noble patron, the Earl of Glencairn, but

received no sinecure. See J. DeLancey Ferguson, *Pride and Passion: Robert Burns* (New York: Oxford University Press, 1939), pp. 98–101.

9. Countess of Loudoun in *The Scots Peerage Founded on Wood's Edition of Sir Robert Douglas's Peerage of Scotland*, ed. Sir James Balfour Paul, LLD, Lord Lyon King of Arms, Edinburgh: D. Douglas, 1904–14. For details of the Loudoun family, see also John Strawhorn, *Ayrshire*, pp. 39–40 and passim.

10. Frank Brady, *James Boswell. The Later Years 1769–1795* (New York: McGraw-Hill, 1984), p. 464.

11. Robert T. Fitzhugh, *Robert Burns: The Man and the Poet. A Round, Unvarnished Account* (Boston: Houghton Mifflin Company, 1970), p. 202. For public support for national leaders, see *Ancient Laws and Customs of the Burghs of Scotland. Burgh Records Society*, preface, p. xlix. For Burns's pro-working class sentiments, see also Thomas Johnston, *The History of the Working Class in Scotland* (Yorkshire: EP Publishing Ltd., Rowman and Littlefield, 1974), p. 61. For the language of patriotism in Britain during the revolutionary decades, see Hugh Cunningham, "The Language of Patriotism," in *Patriotism: The Making and Unmaking of British National Identity*, vol. 1, *History and Politics* (New York: Routledge, 1989), pp. 61–69. Cunningham also refers to contemporary references to King Alfred and to the Norman Yoke, p. 66.

12. I am not suggesting that Little is responding to Burns's poem "For a' That" as it was written after her publication; rather, that his poem encapsulated the sentiments that struck fear in people following the French and San Domingan Revolutions in 1789 and 1791. Burns himself recanted. See T. M. Devine, "The Failure of Radical Reformism in Scotland in the Late Eighteenth Century: The Social and Economic Context," in *Conflict and Stability in Scottish Society. Proceedings of the Scottish Historical Studies Seminar, University of Strathclyde 1988–89*, ed. T. M. Devine (Edinburgh: John Donald Publishers, Ltd., 1990), p. 59.

13. David Craig, *Scottish Literature and The Scottish People 1630–1830* (London: Chatto and Windus, 1961), p. 90. For Burns's views on the French Revolution and reaction to them, see Thomas Johnston, *The History of the Working Class in Scotland*, p. 222.

14. Frances Dunlop comments on Janet Little to Burns on several occasions with a view, it seems, of securing Burns's good opinion of Little. She states that "Jenny Little . . . has wrote some things of late that I would have sent you . . . She says ten guineas would make her as happy as worldly circumstances could do . . . were her rhymes properly put out, as . . . she might be made happy and indebted to none but herself, since her modest wishes are placed within humble bounds" (*Robert Burns and Mrs. Dunlop: Correspondence*, vol. 1, pp. 102–103). DeLancey Ferguson concludes that

Mrs. Dunlop saw "no *essential* difference between [Robert Burns] and Janet Little" (DeLancey Ferguson, *Pride and Passion*, p. 159).

15. *Robert Burns and Mrs. Dunlop: Correspondence*, vol. 1, p. 274. Little might well have been aware of Mrs. Dunlop's superciliousness mixed with concern. She goes on:

> She is industrious, and seems good-temper'd and discreet, but betrays no one indication that I could discover of ever having opened a book or tagged a rhyme; so that I hope she will not be less happy for having tryed it. . . . Tell me what you think of Jenny Little's "Looking Glass." The occasion on which she wrote it was to convince a young lady who doubted the authenticity of her having wrote something else she had shewed her, and asked her to write on a given subject. She said she had never done so, but, since she wished it, would try if she would give her one. She told me she had that forenoon broke a glass she was vext about, and bid her celebrate it.

In another context, Frances Dunlop describes Little to Burns as follows:

> Poor Jenny Little has met a unfortunate accident, which once threatened the loss, if not of life, at least of a limb. I wish her absolute cure be yet a certain expectation, as I understand she still walks with much difficulty. I wish we were ascertained a little time would remove this. Health of body and serenity of mind are distinctions to which it will be very hard if her character and talents cannot attain, since denied the more glaring advantages of life.

Frances Dunlop's view of her own daughter's accident, moreover, is telling in terms of class relations:

> Just the day after I wrote you last, I got an express telling me she was delivered of a dead boy in consequence of a fright she had got by one of the horses falling down in a strong convulsion as she was airing in a carriage about ten days before. Those, my friend, are secured from such accidents who have no carriage. Let us learn to know and mark the advantages of our lot with a gratefully contented heart and a justly distinguishing eye. I had a carriage, but, having also a lame horse, could not use it to fly to my distrest child. (Letter to Robert Burns, September 6, 1789)

16. James Paterson, *The Contemporaries of Burns and The More Recent Poets of Ayrshire* (Edinburgh: Adam Hugh Paton, 1840), p. 83.

17. Craig, *Scottish Literature*, p. 117. For further discussion of the contention that the popularity of vernacular poems is separate from quality, see Carol McGuirk, *Robert Burns and the Sentimental Era* (Athens: University of Georgia Press, 1985), pp. 35–37.

18. Craig, *Scottish Literature*, p. 117.

19. *Robert Burns and Mrs. Dunlop: Correspondence*, p. 80.

20. Craig, *Scottish Literature*, p. 110. For a background to Janet Little's class and the conditions of female laborers, see T. C. Smout, *A History of the Scottish People 1560–1650* (London: Collins, 1969), pp. 302–308.

21. Craig, *Scottish Literature*, p. 129. As a working-class woman, Janet Little's experiences were constrained. Through her friendship with Frances Dunlop, she was also well aware of Burns's own financial difficulties. Donna Landry addresses Little's concerns as a laboring-class woman in *The Muses of Resistance. Laboring-Class Women's Poetry in Britain, 1739–1796* (Cambridge: Cambridge University Press, 1990), pp. 220–57. For a general class context, see also E. P. Thompson, "Patrician Society, Plebian Culture," in *Journal of Social History* (Summer 1974): 382–405. For the general conditions of dairywomen, see Ivy Pinchbeck, *Women Workers and the Industrial Revolution 1750–1850* (New York: F. S. Crofts and Co., 1930), pp. 10–26; for the life of a Scottish dairywoman, see James E. Handley, *The Agricultural Revolution in Scotland*, 1963, pp. 152, 181, 191–92, and passim.

22. Daiches, *Robert Burns*, p. 33. For a full discussion of the religious context of the Scottish Enlightenment, see Richard Sher, *Church and University in the Scottish Englightenment: The Moderate Literati of Edinburgh* (Edinburgh: Edinburgh University Press, 1985). See also Smout, *A History*, especially pp. 229–39.

23. Daiches, *Robert Burns*, p. 12; Henry Grey Graham, *The Social Life of Scotland*, vol. 2 (London: Adam and Charles Black, 1900), p. 256.

24. See *The Works of Allan Ramsay*. Scottish Text Society Edition, 4 vols., 1970.

25. J. DeLancey Ferguson, *The Letters of Robert Burns*, ed. G. Ross Roy, vol. 1 (Oxford: Clarendon Press, 1985), p. 438.

26. It needs also to be noted that Robert Fergusson was one among many Scottish detractors of Samuel Johnson for his mockery in the *Tour*. "To Dr. Samuel Johnson. Food for a New Edition of his Dictionary," in *The Works of Robert Fergusson* (Edinburgh: The Mercat Press, 1970), pp. 203–206.

27. Given the popularity and wide circulation of Johnson's *Lives of the Poets* and the controversay over John Bell's multiple volumes of *The Poets of Great Britain* printed in Edinburgh, Janet Little had easy access to Johnson's *Lives*, if only though Mrs. Dunlop's collection. See Thomas F. Bonnell, "John Bell's *Poets of Great Britain*: The 'Little Trifling Edition,' *Modern Philology*, vol. 85, no. 2 (November 1987), 128–52.

28. Craig, *Scottish Literature*, pp. 57, 62–63.

29. Linda Colley, *Britons: Forging a Nation 1707–1837* (New Haven:

Yale University Press, 1992), p. 117. For background, see Colley's discussion of John Wilkes and Englishness, pp. 105–32.

30. Colley, *Britons*, p. 241.

31. Burns's choice of Pegasus as a fictional name for his horse is curious. Mythologically, Bellerophon defeated the Amazons with Pegasus's help. Perhaps self-mockery enters here, with Burns evoking his attractiveness to women. *The Dictionary of Classical Mythology*, trans. A. R. Maxwell-Hyslop, New York: Blackwell, 1986), p. 349; Adrian Room, *Room's Classical Dictionary. The Origins of the Names of Characters in Classical Mythology* (London: Routledge and Kegan Paul, 1983), p. 231.

32. Daiches, *Robert Burns*, p. 104.

33. *Robert Burns and Mrs. Dunlop: Correspondence*, ed. Wallace, vol. 2, 242.

34. James E. Handley, *Scottish Farming in the Eighteenth Century* (London: Faber and Faber Limited, 1953), p. 71.

35. Paterson, *Contemporaries of Burns*, p. 88.

36. Although Little goes on to state that her wishes and desires are "centre'd all on Him" and attack those whose immoral way of life prevents happiness, her own pleasure in material—as opposed to spiritual—reality is evident both in her poem and (it seems) in her worthy occupation as a dairywoman.

37. Daiches, *Robert Burns*, p. 75. John Ramsay records that Burns referred to himself as a "Jacobite, an Arminian, and a Socinian." John Ramsay, *Scotland and Scotsmen in Eighteenth Century* (Edinburgh and London: William Blackwood and Sons, 1888), p. 554. See also John C. Weston, "Robert Burns's Satire," in *The Art of Robert Burns*, ed. R. D. S. Jack and Andrew Noble (New York: Vision and Barnes and Noble, 1982), p. 53.

38. Craig, *Scottish Literature*, p. 125. In a letter to Mrs. Dunlop, Burns spoke about his "sentiments respecting the present two great Parties that divide our Scots Ecclesiastics.—I do not care three farthings for Commentators and authorities." J. DeLancey Ferguson, *The Letters of Robert Burns*, 2nd ed., vol. 1, p. 422. Note also that Janet Little was a Burgher. For information, see J. H. S. Burleigh, *A Church History of Scotland* (London: Oxford University Press, 1960), p. 323.

39. Fitzhugh, *Robert Burns*, p. 68.

40. Previously the Kirk Session had denounced Gavin Hamilton, Burns's friend and landlord, for "breaking the Sabbath" and for "contumacy."Little mentions Gavin Hamilton somewhat ambiguously in her poem about the Scottish literary tradition, "Given to a Lady." In "Holy Willie's Prayer," Burns ridiculed this censure that Hamilton subsequently and suc-

cessfully appealed. This title appears only in the Alloway ms. The other title is "A Poet's Welcome to his love-begotten Daughter" (Glenriddell ms.); "Address to an Illegitimate Child" (Stewart, 1801). Thomas Crawford discusses Burns's response in verse to religious controversies in Mauchline Parish in *Burns: A Study of the Poems and Songs* (Stanford: Stanford University Press, 1960), pp. 67–69. Note also that Burns supported the child he had with Elizabeth Paton before his marriage. The child was reared by his mother. He had at least three subsequent children with other women while he was married to Jean Armour. The two daughters who survived were reared in his own family. In "The Court of Equity," Burns discussed male responsibility in sexual matters outside marriage. Although there is abundant evidence to suggest that Burns's sexual relationships were consensual, Little seems to assume a very traditional view of Burns's relationships, not unlike the early view tendered by Jean Armour's parents. Note further negative narratives about Burns's public behavior are manufactured after his political opinions became controversial. See Donald Low, ed., *Robert Burns: The Critical Heritage* (London: Routledge and Kegan Paul, 1974).

41. I am indebted here and elsewhere in the chapter to David Morris's study of Burns's poems from a Bakhtinian point of view, especially the idea that conflict in diction bespeaks social conflict. David Morris, "Burns and Heteroglossia," in *The Eighteenth Century: Theory and Interpretation* (Winter, 1987), pp. 3–27.

42. *Princeton Encyclopedia of Poetry and Poetics*, ed. Alex Preminger (Princeton: Princeton University Press, 1965), p. 606.

43. Eric Smith, *A Dictionary of Classical Reference in English Poetry* (Cambridge: D. S. Brewer, 1984), p. 76.

44. See Morris, "Burns and Heteroglossia"; see also Alexander Warrack, *Scots Dictionary Serving as a Glossary for Ramsay, Fergusson, Burns, Galt, Minor Poets, Kailyard Novelists, and a Host of Other Writers of the Scottish Tongue* (University of Alabama Press, 1911, reprint. 1965), p. 427; and William Graham, *The Scots Word Book* (Edinburgh: The Ramsay Head Press, 1977), p. 165.

45. Burns's relationship to women has frequently been distorted due to inaccuracies in an earlier biography by James Currie. In 1793, he is also said to have given verbal offense to Elizabeth Riddell, wife of Robert Riddell, hosts at a dinner party at Woodley Park, the home of Walter and Maria Riddell. Maria was born in 1772 and was famous for *Voyages to the Madeira and Leeward Caribbean Islands* (Edinburgh: Peter Hill, 1792). Burns was rumored to be having an affair with her. The Riddell family cold-shouldered Burns from then on, despite Burns's letter of apology sent the following day. Maria Riddell speaks of once asking Burns why he had never learned Latin. Burns replied that "he already knew all the Latin he desired to learn, and that was "Omnia vincit amor": a phrase, Maria adds, "he was most thor-

oughly versed in" (Hugh S. Gladstone, "Maria Riddell, the Friend of Burns," in *Dumfriesshire and Galloway Natural History and Antiquarian Society. Transactions and Journal of Proceedings 1914–15*, Third Series, volume 3., ed. G. W. Shirley [Dumfries: Published by the Council of the Society, 1915], pp. 16–56). See *The Letters of Robert Burns*, 2nd ed., edited by G. Ross Roy (1985), vol. 2, p. 473, for a convincing argument that Elizabeth Riddell was the woman who took offense. For a reevaluation of Currie's biography, see Fitzhugh, *Robert Burns*, especially pp. 91–111.

46. In 1737, Janet Little's parish kirk in Galston, south of the River Irvine, became part of a Scottish-style secession from the Church of Scotland, led by the Reverend Ebenezer Erskine. For historical and geographical details about Galston and Erskine, see Robert Chambers, *A Biographical Dictionary of Eminent Scotsman*, new ed., ed. Thomas Thomson (New York: Georg Olms Verlag, 1855; reprint. 1971). See also *Encyclopaedia Brittanica*, pp. 538–39.

47. John Strawhorn, *Ayrshire at the Time of Burns*, p. 142. See also William Ferguson, *Scotland 1689–the Present* (New York: Praeger, 1968), pp. 118, 122–27; George S. Pryde, *Scotland from 1603 to the Present Day* (London: Thomas Nelson, 1962), pp. 181–82.

48. *Robert Burns and Mrs. Dunlop: Correspondence*, pp. xiv-xv.

49. 'When in 1760 Thomas Wright eloped to Scotland with his wife-to-be, he stayed in an inn. One of the servant girls offered to become their servant. She told them "she could milk the cows, tend and clean them or other cattle, look after the dairy, and upon occasion, do any genteeler work." As Wright added, "I do believe if we had ventured to bring her, she would have made an excellent servant"' (Bridget Hill, *Women, Work, and Sexual Politics in Eighteenth-Century England* [Oxford: Basil Blackwell, 1989], p. 135).

50. Hill, *Women, Work and Sexual Politics*, p. 146; see also Fitzhugh, *Robert Burns*, p. 70.

51. William Auld, the minister of the Mauchline Kirk, Robert Burns's parish, for over fifty years, was a particularly ardent Calvinist. His death might explain the drastic reduction in field communions from 1,400 in 1776 to 400 in 1819.

52. Fitzhugh, *Robert Burns*, p. 75. For Burns's relationship with women, see also Hilton Brown, *There Was a Lad* (London: Hamish Hamilton, 1949), especially pp. 103–65.

53. Landry, *Muses of Resistance*, pp. 220–37.

54. Janet Little, for example, had no access to the cultural society of freemasons, with its secret and comforting promotion of comradely feeling and tacit sympathy among like-minded members. See Douglas Knoop, *An*

Introduction to Freemasonry (Manchester: Manchester University Press, 1937). See also *Oxford English Dictionary*, vol. 6, p. 167.

55. Janet Little's identification with Robert Burns is always, at least, on the basis of their relatively similar class backgrounds. The poverty Burns experienced growing up and his consequent efforts to help class equals like Little is well documented in John C. Weston, "Robert Burns's Satire," in *The Art of Robert Burns*, ed. R. D. S. Jack and Andrew Noble, p. 53.

56. See the Janet Nichol poem (p. 173) and "To the Public," p. 29. If she were Janet Nichol, she would have no such dilemma. In her poem to Nichol, rather ambiguously entitled "A Poem on Contentment. Inscribed to Janet Nichol, a Poor Old Wandering Woman, Who Lives by the Wall at Loudoun and Used Sometimes to Be Visited by the Countess," Little addresses her namesake Janet Nichol and imbricates her dilemma as a woman and as a poet. Little informs Nichol how lucky she is to avoid snares set for females. In particular, she congratulates her for never feeling the pain "we heedless scribbling fools sustain."

57. *Robert Burns and Mrs. Dunlop: Correspondence*, p. 96.

58. In critiquing her poems, Robert Burns may well have been trying to help her. He operated similarly toward male poet-friends, virtually rewriting John Lapraik's poetry. It is also possible that Burns's relationship to Little was part of his complex relationship with Mrs. Dunlop. Little may have been unwittingly caught in the middle.

59. *Robert Burns and Mrs. Dunlop: Correspondence*, p. 137.

60. Unlike Ann Yearsley, however, she appears to cultivate her patrons, and this in turn enables her to challenge critics less acrimoniously.

61. Little, for example, finds some alternative ways of relating to the men and women around her, most notably through tender friendships. Peppering her volume with poems to friends, she acknowledges that while happiness continually eludes us like disappearing "snows on Ailsa falling," love for a friend is incomparable. Hence separation is one of the sharpest pains:

> I have lost no valu'd charter,
> Nor lament a fickle swain;
> But, alas! a friend's departure,
> Fills my heart with piercing pain.
>
> Pond'ring sharpens ev'ry arrow,
> Sighing but augments my grief:
> Now I mourn, o'erwhelm'd with sorrow,
> But next hour May bring relief. (P. 105)

CHAPTER SEVEN

1. I thank Donna Landry for her insights on this issue.

2. Linda Colley *Britons: Forging the Nation 1707–1837* (New Haven: Yale University Press, 1992), p. 52.

3. See Cheryl A. Wall, *Changing Our Own Words: Essays on Criticism, Theory, and Writing by Black Women* (New Brunswick: Rutgers University Press, 1989), p. 6.

BIBLIOGRAPHY

PRIMARY SOURCES

Collier, Mary. *The Poems of Mary Collier, the Washerwoman of Petersfield; To which is prefixed her Life, Drawn by Herself. A New Edition* (Petersfield: Printed and Published by W. Minchin; and Sold by all Booksellers, 1762).

———. *"The Woman's Labour: An Epistle to Mr. Stephen Duck; In Answer to his late Poem, called The Thresher's Labour* (London, 1739).

———. *The Woman's Labour* in *The Thresher's Labour* and *The Woman's Labour*, intro. Moira Ferguson (Los Angeles: University of California Press, 1985).

Little, Janet. *The Poetical Works of Janet Little. The Scotch Milkmaid* (Ayr: John and Peter Wilson, 1792).

Scott, Mary. *The Female Advocate* (London: Joseph Johnson, 1774; rpt. ed. and intro. Gae Holladay, Augustan Reprints Society, No. 224).

———. *The Female Advocate; A Poem. Occasioned by Reading Mr. Duncombe's Feminead (1774)* (Los Angeles: University of California Press, 1984).

———. *Messiah: A Poem. In Two Parts. Published for the benefit of the General Hospital at Bath* (Bath, 1788).

Yearsley, Ann. "An Elegy on Marie Antoinette of Austria, ci-devant queen of France: with a poem on the last interview between the King of Poland and Loraski." (Printed by J. Rudhall and sold by the author, at her library, Hotwells: and by the principal booksellers in Bristol, Bath, etc., 1795?).

———. *Poems on Several Occasions* (London: T. Cadell, 1785).

———. *Poems on Various Subjects* (London: Printed for the Author, and Sold by G. G. J. and J. Robinson, 1787).

————. "Reflections on the death of Louis XVI." (Bristol: Printed for, and sold by the author, at her public-library, Crescent, Hotwells, n.d.).

————. *Rural Lyre: A Volume of Poems* (London: G. G. J. and J. Robinson, 1796).

————. "The Unpublished Poems of Ann Yearsley." Edited by Moira Ferguson. *Tulsa Studies in Women's Literature*, vol. 12, no. 1, Spring 1993.

SECONDARY SOURCES: BOOKS

The Anchor Bible. I and II Esdras, intro. trans., and commentary Jacob M. Myers (New York: Doubleday, 1974).

Ancient Laws and Customs of the Burghs of Scotland. Burgh Records Society, Preface.

Anderson, Benedict. *Imagined Communities: Reflections on the Origin and Spread of Nationalism*. London: Verso, 1983.

Ashton, T. S. *An Economic History of England: The 18th Century* (London: Methuen and Co., 1955).

Ayling, Stanley. *George the Third*, vols. 1 and 2. (New York: Alfred A. Knopf, 1972).

Ballard, George. *Memoirs of Several Ladies of Great Britain Who Have Been Celebrated for Their Writings or Skill in the Learned Languages* (Oxford: W. Jackson, 1752).

Bell, Groag, and Karen M. Offen, eds. *Women, the Family and Freedom*, vol. 1, 1750–1880 (Stanford, CA: Stanford University Press, 1983).

Benger, Elizabeth. *The Female Geniad: A Poem* (London, 1791).

Bentham, Matilda. *Biographical Dictionary of the Celebrated Women of Every Age and Country* (1804).

Bibliotheca Somersetensis (London, 1902).

Biographeum Femineum. The Female Worthies: or Memoirs of the Most Illustrious Ladies of All Ages and Nations, 2 vols. (London, 1766).

Biographia Dramatica; or, a Companion to the Playhouse, etc., ed. D. E. Baker, I. Reed, and Stephen Jones. 3 vols. Republished Graz, Austria: Akademische Druck u. Verlagsanstalt, 1967.

Black, Jeremy, ed. *Britain in the Age of Walpole* (New York: Macmillan, 1984).

Boccaccio, Giovanni. *De Claris Mulieribus [Concerning Famous Women]*, trans. G. A. Guarino (New Brunswick, NJ: Rutgers University Press, 1963).

Brady, Frank. *James Boswell: The Later Years 1769–1795* (New York: McGraw-Hill Book Company, 1984).

Brant, Clare and Diane Purkiss, eds. *Women, Texts, and Histories 1575–1760*, London: Routledge, 1992.

Brewer, John. *The Sinews of Nation, War, Money and the State* (London: Unwin Hyman, 1989).

Brooke, John. *King George III* (New York: McGraw-Hill, 1972).

Brown, Hilton. *There Was a Lad: An Essay on Robert Burns* (London: Hamish Hamilton, 1949).

Burleigh, J. H. S. *A Church History of Scotland* (London: Oxford University Press, 1960).

Robert Burns and Mrs. Dunlop. Correspondence Now Published in Full for the First Time, ed. William Wallace. 2 vols. (New York: Dodd, Mead and Company, 1898).

Catalogue of the Books, Tracts, etc. contained in Ann Yearsley's Public Library. No. 4, Crescent, Hotwells. (Bristol, 1793).

Chambers, Robert. *A Biographical Dictionary of Eminent Scotsmen*, new ed. Edited by Thomas Thomson (New York: Georg Olms Verlag, 1855; reprint. 1971).

Chapone, Hester Mulso. *The Posthumous Works of Mrs. Chapone containing her correspondence with Mr. Richardson*, 2 vols. (London: John Murray, 1807).

Chatterton, Lady Georgiana. *Memorials. . . of Admiral Lord Gambier* (London, 1861). (Correspondence with Lady Middleton.)

Chaucer, Geoffrey. *Legend of Good Women* (c. 1380–1386). *The Complete Works of Geoffrey Chaucer*, ed. F. N. Robinson (Oxford: Oxford University Press, 1933).

Christie, Thomas, and Joseph Johnson, eds. *The Analytical Review or History of Literature, Domestic and Foreign, or an Enlarged Plan. Containing Scientific Abstracts of Important and Interesting Works, Published in English; A General Account of such as are of Less Consequence, with Short Characters; Notices, or Reviews, or Valuable Foreign Books; Criticisms on New Pieces of Music and Works of Art; and the Literary Intelligence of Europe, etc.* (London: Joseph Johnson, 1788).

Chudleigh, Lady Mary. *The Ladies Defence; or, "The Bride-Woman's Counsellor" answer'd: a poem* (London: for John Deeve, 1701).

Cibber, Theophilus. *An Account of the Lives of the Poets of Great Britain and Ireland*, 4 vols. (London, 1753).

Coleman, George, and Bonnell Thornton, eds. *Poems by Eminent Ladies* (London: R. Baldwin, 1755).

Colley, Linda. *Britons: Forging the Nation* (New Haven: Yale University Press, 1992).

Collins, A. S. *Authorship in the Days of Johnson: Being a Study of the Relation beween Author, Patron, Publisher, and Public, 1726–1780* (London: Robert Holden, 1927).

The Complete Peerage of George Edward Cokayne, revised and enlarged by Vicary Gibbs, vol. 8 (London: St. Catherine Press, 1932).

Craig, David. *Scottish Literature and the Scottish People 1630–1830* (London: Chatto and Windus, 1961).

Crawford, Thomas. *Burns: A Study of the Poems and Songs* (Stanford: Stanford University Press, 1960).

The Critical Review: or, Annals of Literature (London: A Hamilton, 1774).

Daiches, David. *Robert Burns* (New York: Macmillan, 1966).

A Dictionary of Philosophy, ed. Antony Flew (New York: St. Martin's Press, 1979).

Douglas, Ronald MacDonald. *The Scots Book of Lore and Folklore* (New York: Beekman House, 1982).

Edwards, Paul, and James Walvin. *Black Personalities in the Era of the Slave Trade* (Baton Rouge, Louisiana State University Press, 1983).

Ferguson, J. DeLancy. *The Letters of Robert Burns*, ed. G. Ross Roy, vol. 2 (Oxford: Clarendon Press, 1985).

Ferguson, Moira, ed. *First Feminists: British Women Writers 1578–1799* (Bloomington: Indiana University Press and New York: The Feminist Press, 1985).

———. *Subject to Others: British Women Writers and Colonial Slavery, 1678–1834* (New York: Routledge, 1992).

Findlay, H. L. *A Book of Scotland* (London and Glasgow: Collins, n.d.).

Fitzhugh, Robert T. *Robert Burns: The Man and the Poet. A Round, Unvarnished Account* (Boston: Houghton Mifflin Company, 1970).

Fletcher, Eliza Dawson. *Autobiography of Mrs. Fletcher, with Letters and Other Family Memorials*. Edited by the Survivors of her Family. 3rd edition. Edinburgh: Edmonston and Douglas, 1876.

Fryer, Peter. *Staying Power: The History of Black People in Britain* (London, 1984).

Fussell, G. E. *The English Dairy Farmer* (New York: Augustus M. Kelley, 1966).

Garrett, Richard. *General Wolfe* (London: Arthur Baker Limited, 1975).

Gelpi, Barbara Charlesworth, and Albert Gelpi, eds. *Adrienne Rich's Poetry: Texts of the Poems. The Poet on Her Work. Reviews and Criticisms*, ed. Barbara Charlesworth Gelpi and Albert Gelpi (New York: W. W. Norton and Company, Inc., 1975).

The Gentleman's Magazine, and Historical Chronicle, vol. 44 (London, 1774).

George, Dorothy M. *London Life in the Eighteenth Century* (New York: Capricorn, 1965).

Gerbier, Charles. *Elogium Heroinum. The Ladies Vindication; or, The Praise of Worthy Women* (London, 1651).

Graham, Henry Grey. *The Social Life of Scotland*, vol. 2 (London: Adam and Charles Black, 1900).

Graham, William. *The Scots Word Book* (Edinburgh: The Ramsay Head Press, 1977).

Grimal, Pierre. *The Dictionary of Classical Mythology*, trans. A. R. Maxwell-Hyslop (New York: Blackwell, 1986).

Grinnell-Milne, Duncan. *Mad, Is He? The Character and Achievement of James Wolfe* (London: Bodley Head, 1963).

Handley, James E. *Scottish Farming in the Eighteenth Century* (London: Faber and Faber Limited, 1953).

Hays, Mary. *Female Biography; or Memoirs of Illustrious and Celebrated Women, of All Ages and Countries. Alphabetically Arranged*, 6 vols., vol. 3 (London: Printed for Richard Phillips, 71, St. Paul's Church-Yard. By Thomas Davison, White-Friars, 1803).

Hesselgrave, Ruth Avaline. *Lady Miller and the Batheaston Literary Circle* (New Haven, Yale University Press, 1927).

Heywood, Thomas. *Gynaikeion: or Nine Books of Various History, concerning Women* (London, 1624, 1657).

Hill, Bridget. *Eighteenth-Century Women: An Anthology* (London: Allen and Unwin, 1984).

———. *The Republican Virago: The Life and Times of Catharine Macaulay, Historian* (Oxford: Clarendon Press, 1992).

———. *Women, Work, and Sexual Politics in Eighteenth-Century England* (Oxford: Basil Blackwell, 1989).

Hill, Christopher. *Reformation to Industrial Revolution: The Pelican Economic History of Britain* (London: Penguin Books, 1967).

The History of Churcher's College, Petersfield, Hants, with a Sketch of the Life of Mr. Richard Churcher, The Founder; and Observations of its Management: together with a Report of the Case now pending in the High Court of Chancery,

Between the Trustees and Several of the Inhabitants of Petersfield (London: Joseph Butterworth and Son, Fleet Street, Wm. Minchin, Petersfield; and all other booksellers, 1823).

Hobsbawm, E. J. *Industry and Europe: The Pelican Economic History of Britain* (London: Penguin Books, 1968).

Hobsbawm, Eric, and Terence Ranger. *The Invention of Tradition* (Cambridge: Cambridge University Press, 1983).

Hughes, Helen Sard. *The Gentle Hertford: Her Life and Letters* (New York, 1940).

Hurt-Mead, Kate. *A History of Women in Medicine from the Earliest Times to the Beginning of the 19th Century* (Haddam, CN: The Haddam Press, 1938).

Jack, R. D. S., ed. *The Art of Robert Burns* (New York: Vision and Barnes and Noble, 1982).

Johnson, R. Brimley, ed. *Bluestocking Letters* (London: John Lane, 1926).

Johnston, Thomas. *The History of the Working Classes in Scotland* (Yorkshire: EP Publishing Ltd., Rowman and Littlefield, 1974).

Jones, M. G. *Hannah More* (Cambridge: Cambridge University Press, 1952).

Kelly, Linda. *The Marvellous Boy: The Life and Myth of Thomas Chatterton* (London: Weidenfeld and Nicolson, 1971).

Kinsley, James, ed. *The Poems and Songs of Robert Burns*, vol. 3 (Oxford: Clarendon Press, 1968).

Knoop, Douglas. *An Introduction to Freemasonry* (Manchester: Manchester University Press, 1937).

Landry, Donna. *The Muses of Resistance: Laboring-Class Women's Poetry in Britain 1739–1796* (Cambridge: Cambridge University Press, 1990).

The Letters of Robert Burns, ed. J. de Lancey Ferguson. 2d ed. ed. G. Ross Roy, vol. 1, 1780–1789, vol. 2, 1790–1796 (Oxford: Clarendon Press, 1985).

Lindsay, Maurice. *The Burns Encyclopedia* (New York: St. Martin's Press; London: Robert Hale, 1959).

———. *Robert Burns: The Man, His Work, the Legend* (London: Macgibbon and Kee, 1954).

Lonsdale, Roger, ed. *Eighteenth Century Women Poets: An Oxford Anthology* (Oxford: Oxford University Press, 1990).

Loughhead, Flora Haines. *Dictionary of Given Names with Origins and Meanings* (Glendale, CA: The Arthur H. Clark Company, 1958).

Low, Donald, ed. *Robert Burns: The Critical Heritage* (London: Routledge and Kegan Paul, 1974).

Macintosh, John. *The Poets of Ayrshire from the Fourteenth Century Till the Present Day* (Dumfries: Thos. Hunter and Co., n.d.).

Mackie, J. D. *A History of Scotland* (Middlesex: Penguin Books Ltd., 1964).

Mahl, Mary, and Helene Koon. *The Female Spectator: English Women Writers before 1800* (Bloomington: The Feminist Press, 1977).

Maitland, S. R. *Chatterton: An Essay* (London: Folcroft Library Editions, 1972; Facsimile of 1857 Rivingtons, Waterloo Place ed.).

Makin, Bathsua. *An Essay to Revive the Antient Education of Gentlewomen* (London: J. Deeve, 1673; rpt., ed. and introd. by Paula L. Barbour, Augustan Reprints Society, No. 202).

Mavor, Elizabeth. *The Ladies of Llangollen: A Study in Romantic Friendship* (London: Michael Joseph, 1971).

McGuirk, Carol. *Robert Burns and the Sentimental Era* (Athens: University of Georgia Press, 1985).

The Monthly Review: or, Literary Journal, vol. 51 (London, 1774).

Myers, Sylvia Harcstark. *The Bluestocking Circle: Women, Friendship, and the Life of the Mind in Eighteenth-Century England* (Oxford: Clarendon Press, 1990).

Newman, Gerald. *The Rise of English Nationalism: A Cultural History, 1740–1830* (New York: St. Martin's Press, 1987).

Noble, Andrew, ed. *The Art of Robert Burns* (New York: Vision and Barnes and Noble, 1982).

Paterson, James. *The Contemporaries of Burns and the More Recent Poets of Ayrshire* (Edinburgh: Adam Hugh Paton, 1840).

Perry, Ruth. *The Celebrated Mary Astell: An Early English Feminist* (Chicago, University of Chicago Press, 1986).

Pinchbeck, Ivy. *Women Workers and the Industrial Revolution 1750–1850* (New York: F. S. Crofts and Co., 1930).

Pisan, Christine de. *La Cité des Dames* (c. 1405), trans. Bryan Anslay (London, 1521).

Plant, Marjorie. *The Domestic Life of Scotland in the Eighteenth Century* (Edinburgh: Edinburgh University Press, 1952).

Plutarch. *Moralia,* ed. and trans. F. C. Babbitt, H. Cherniss, et al. 2 vols. (London, New York and Cambridge, MA: Loeb Classical Library, 1927–).

Poovey, Mary. *The Proper Lady and The Woman Writer: Ideology as Style in the Works of Mary Wollstonecraft, Mary Shelley, and Jane Austen* (Chicago and London: The University of Chicago Press, 1984).

Porter, Roy. *English Society in the Eighteenth Century*, in *The Pelican Social History of Britain* (London: Penguin Books, 1982).

Princeton Encyclopedia of Poetry and Poetics, ed. Alex Preminger (Princeton: Princeton University Press, 1965).

Prior, Mary, ed. Women in English Society, 1500–1800 (London: Methuen, 1985).

Ramsay, John. *Scotland and Scotsmen in the Eighteenth Century* (Edinburgh and London: William Blackwood and Sons, 1888).

Reed, John. *The New Bristol Directory, For the Year 1792, Containing An Historical and Commercial Account of the Rise, Progress, and Present State of that City, with its Manufactures, Home and Foreign, Trade, Shipping, etc. Also, an Alphabetical List of the Corporation, Gentry, Clergy, Merchants, Bankers, Professors of Law and Physic, Manufacturers, and Traders, in the City, Suburbs, and Hotwells; with Lists of the Mail and Other Coaches, Waggons, Coasting Vessels, Trows, Market Boats, and Navigation Barges, by which Goods and Merchandise are Conveyed from this City the Sea Severn or Inland Navigation to every part of the kingdom. Particulars of the Coming In and Going Out of the Posts, Home and Foreign, with the Custom-House, Excise Office, etc. Also, A List of the Hackney Coaches, and Their Legal Fares. To Which Is Added, An Historical Account of the Hot-wells in their ancient and present State; and a Description of the Seats, Villages, and Curiosities, in the adjacent Country, with Directions for Crossing the Aust. and New Passage with Safety* (Bristol: Printed for and Sold by Wm. Browne, et al.), especially for 1775, 1785, 1793–94.

Riddell, Walter, and Maria Riddell. *Voyages to the Madeira and Leeward Caribbean Islands* (Edinburgh: Peter Hill, 1792).

Roberts, William. *Memoirs of the Life and Correspondence of Mrs. Hannah More*, 4 vols. (London: R. B. Seeley and W. Burnside, 1834).

Room, Adrian. *Room's Classical Dictionary. The Origins of the Names of Characters in Classical Mythology* (London: Routledge and Kegan Paul, 1983).

Ross, John E. *Who's Who in Burns* (Stirling: Eneas Mackay, 1927).

Roy, G. Ross. *The Letters of Robert Burns* (Oxford: Clarendon Press, 1985).

Rudé, George. *Wilkes and Liberty* (London: Lawrence and Wishart, 1962).

Sahakian, William S. *History of Philosophy* (New York: Barnes and Noble Books, 1968).

The Scots Peerage Founded on Wood's Edition of Sir Robert Douglas's Peerage of Scotland, ed. Sir James Balfour Paul (Edinburgh: D. Douglas, 1904–14).

Scott, Sarah. *A Description of Millenium Hall and the Country Adjacent: together with the Characters of the Inhabitants, and such Historical Anecdotes and Reflections, as may excite in the Reader proper Sentiments of Humanity, and lead the Mind to the Love of Virtue. By A Gentleman on his Travels* (London: for T. Carnan, 1762).

Seward, Anna. *Letters of Anna Seward Written Between the Years 1784 and 1807,* vol. 3 (Edinburgh: Printed by George Ramsay and Company for Archibald Constable, et al., 1811).

Seward, Thomas. "The Female Right to Literature." In *A Collection of Poems in Three Volumes by Several Hands* (London: J. Hughes, 1751).

Sher, Richard. *Church and University in the Scottish Enlightenment: The Moderate Literati of Edinburgh* (Edinburgh: Edinburgh University Press, 1985).

Skillington, Florence E. *The Coltmans of the Newarke at Leicester* in *Transactions of the Leicestershire Archaelogical Society* (Leicester: W. Thornley and Son, 1934–35).

Smith, Eric. *A Dictionary of Classical References in English Poetry* (Cambridge: D. S. Brewer, 1984).

Smith, Hilda L. *Reason's Disciples: Seventeenth-Century English Feminists* (Urbana: University of Illinois Press, 1982).

Smout, T. C. *A History of the Scottish People 1560–1650* (London: Collins, 1969).

Southey, Robert. *The Lives and Works of the Uneducated Poets,* ed. J. S. Childers (London, 1925).

Sprint, John. *The Bride-Womans Counsellor, Being a Sermon Preach'd at a Wedding, May the 11th, 1699, at Sherbourn, in Dorsetshire* (London: H. Hills, 1699).

Stadter, Philip A. *Plutarch's Historical Methods: An Analysis of the Mulierum Virtutes* (Cambridge: Harvard University Press, 1965).

Stecher, Henry F. *Elizabeth Singer Rowe: The Poetess of Frome: A Study of Eighteenth-Century English Pietism* (Frankfurt, 1973).

Stone, Lawrence. *The Family, Sex, and Marriage in England 1500–1800* (London: Weidenfeld and Nicolson, 1977).

Strawhorn, John. *Ayrshire at the Time of Burns* (Ayr: Archaelogical Natural History Society, 1959).

Sykes, Egerton. *Everyman's Dictionary of Non-Classical Mythology* (London: J. M. Dent and Sons, n.d.).

Thirsk, Joan. *Agricultural Regions and Agrarian History in England, 1500–1750* (London: Macmillan Education, 1987).

Tilly, Louise A., and Joan W. Scott. *Women, Work, and Family* (New York: Holt, Rinehart and Winston, 1978).

Tinker, Chauncy Brewster. *Nature's Simple Plan: A Phase of Radical Thought in the Mid-Eighteenth Century* (Princeton, 1922).

Tollett, Elizabeth. *Poems on Several Occasions with Anne Boleyn to King Henry VIII. An Epistle* (London: John Clarke, 1755).

Trevelyan, G. M. *History of England* (Garden City: Doubleday and Company, Inc., 1926).

Turner, Cheryl, *Living by the Pen: Women Writers in the Eighteenth Century*, New York: Routledge, 1992.

Unwin, Rayner. *The Rural Muse: Studies in the Peasant Poetry of England* (London, 1954).

Valenze, Deborah M. *Prophetic Sons and Daughters* (Princeton, NJ: Princeton University Press, 1985).

Wall, Cheryl A. *Changing Our Own Words. Essays on Criticism, Theory, and Writing by Black Women* (New Brunswick and London: Rutgers University Press, 1989).

Warrack, Alexander. *Scots Dictionary serving as a glossary for Ramsay, Fergusson, Burns, Galt, minor poets, kailyard novelists, and a host of other writers of the Scottish tongues* (University of Alabama Press, 1911, rpt. 1965).

Warren, Murray. *A Description and Annotated Bibliography of Thomas Chatterton* (New York and London: Garland Publishing, Inc., 1977).

Williams, Raymond. *The Country and the City* (New York: Oxford University Press, 1973).

Wollstonecraft, Mary. *A Vindication of the Rights of Women* (London: Joseph Johnson, 1791).

Wrightson, Keith. *English Society 1580–1680* (London: Hutchinson, 1982).

Young, James D. *Women and Popular Struggles: A History of British Working-class Women, 1560–1984* (Edinburgh: Mainstream Publishing, 1985).

SECONDARY SOURCES: ARTICLES

Blanchard, Rae. "Richard Steele and the Status of Women," (*North Carolina Press, Studies in Philology*, 26 July 1929, no. 3.

Bonnell, Thomas F. "John Bell's *Poets of Great Britain*: The 'Little Trifling Edition,' *Modern Philology*, vol. 85, no. 2 (November 1987).

Davis, Rose Mary. "Stephen Duck, The Thresher-Poet," *University of Maine Studies*, 2d Series, No. 8 (Orono, Maine: University Press, 1926).

Devine, T. M., ed. "The Failure of Radical Reformism in Scotland in the Late Eighteenth Century: The Social and Economic Context," *Conflict and Stability in Scottish Society 1700–1850. Proceedings of the Scottish Historical Studies Seminar, University of Strathcyle 1988–89* (Edinburgh: John Donald Publishers, Ltd., 1990).

Ferguson, Moira. "Resistance and Power in the Life and Writings of Ann Yearsley," in *Eighteenth-Century Theory and Interpretation* 27, 3 (1986).

Gladstone, Hugh S. "Maria Riddell, the Friend of Burns," in *Dumfriesshire and Galloway Natural History and Antiquarian Society. Transactions and Journal of Proceedings 1914–15*, ed. G. W. Shirley. 3d Series, vol. 3 (Dumfries: Published by the Council of the Society, 1915).

Hampsten, Elizabeth. "Petticoat Authors: 1660–1720." *Women's Studies* 5, 1/2 (1980).

"An Historical Milkwoman," *Chamber's Journal*, n.d., rpt. *The Eclectic Magazine*, March 1856.

Kinghorn, A. M. "The Literary and Historical Origins of the Burns Myth," *Dalhousie Review*, 39, 1959.

Law, Alexander. "Scottish Schoolbooks of the Eighteenth and Nineteenth Centuries," *Studies in Scottish Literature*, ed. G. Ross Roy, vol. 28 (Columbia: University of South Carolina, 1983).

McBurney, William H. "Edmund Curll, Mrs. Jane Barker, and the English Novel," *Philological Quarterly* 37 (1958).

Middleton, Chris. "Women's Labour and the Transition to Pre-Industrial Capitalism," in *Women and Work in Pre-Industrial England*, eds. Lindsey Charles and Lorna Duffin (London: Croom Helm, 1985).

Morris, David B. "Burns and Heteroglossia," in *The Eighteenth Century: Theory and Interpretation* (Winter, 1987).

Perry, Ruth. "The Veil of Chastity: Mary Astell's Feminism." *Studies in Eighteenth Century Culture* 9 (1979).

Stone, Lawrence. "The Rise of the Nuclear Family in Early Modern England: The Patriarchal Stage," in *The Family in History*, ed. Charles E. Rosenberg (Philadelphia: University of Pennsylvania Press, 1975).

Thompson, E. P. "Patrician Society, Plebeian Culture," in *Journal of Social History* (Summer, 1974).

Tompkins, J. M. S. "The Bristol Milkwoman," in *The Polite Marriage: Eighteenth-Century Essays* (Cambridge, 1938).

Waldron, Mary. "Ann Yearsley and the Clifton Records," *Age of Johnson*, vol. 3, (1990).

Weston, John C. "Robert Burns's Satire," *The Art of Robert Burns*, ed. R. D. S. Jack and Andrew Noble (New York: Vision and Barnes and Noble, 1982).

INDEX